CECILIA

Blagdon Hall

CECILIA

THE LIFE AND LETTERS OF
CECILIA RIDLEY
1819 - 1845

Edited by
Ursula Ridley

Preface by
The Viscount Ridley

THE SPREDDEN PRESS
STOCKSFIELD 1990

First published by Rupert Hart-Davis, 1958

This edition published 1990 by
The Spredden Press
Brocksbushes Farm
Stocksfield
Northumberland NE45 7WB

Printed and bound by
SMITH SETTLE
Ilkley Road, Otley, West Yorkshire LS21 3JP

PREFACE

I am delighted that my mother's book about Cecilia Ridley is being republished after so many years. I know what a tremendous labour it was deciphering these generally undated and often illegible letters to piece together one of the most interesting accounts of family history in the North of England. The story is not only short and dramatic, but also a tragedy, with the loss of Cecilia's sister, her third son in infancy, and her own early death in a few years. The Victorians accepted these disasters more philosophically than we would now.

Cecilia has 'to pluck up courage to call her husband by his Christian name' while making penetrating and often indiscreet comments on her neighbours and those she met in the course of her very young life. One notes, for instance, that 'one of the attorneys who did the Ridley business' was 'thin and sickly, something like the Duke of Bedford', and the barristers at the Assizes were 'a very snobby, shabby, sloppy looking set compared with those at York'. It is all delightfully recorded.

I long to know what Cecilia might have said or done had she lived longer, and what a contribution she could have made to Blagdon and North Country life in the latter half of the nineteenth century. I am sure she would have been able to patch up the endless family vendettas which form such a striking theme throughout the book, and she would have outwitted her terrible mother-in-law.

If all the events she wrote about had not actually happened, one could have thought they were the invention of one of the more imaginative Victorian novelists. One thing we can be very grateful for is that the telephone did not exist in the 1840s. I am sure that, if it had, mother and daughter would have spent hours on it nightly and we would have been denied these wonderful letters. Probably no one will ever write such letters again about such, at the time, mundane but now fascinating details.

I hope this new edition will give pleasure to many who have not read the original and I know how pleased my mother would have been to know of the republication of her book.

RIDLEY
Blagdon, June 1990

Contents

Illustrations

Preface

THIS book consists of a small selection from a vast number of letters written by my husband's great-grandmother. They were inherited from her mother by her youngest sister, Alice, who married William Lowther, nephew of the second Earl of Lonsdale. Alice's son, Viscount Ullswater, and her grandson, the Honourable Arthur Lowther, returned the letters piecemeal and at various times to the Ridley home at Blagdon in Northumberland, where they remained unread for many years. In 1952 the discovery of the journals Cecilia kept before her marriage prompted me to undertake the task of sorting the letters.

It proved most difficult to put them into chronological sequence. In addition to the maddening custom of crossing, to which Cecilia was much given, only one of them is dated, nor is there any indication of where they were written in the form of letterhead or address. Not even the type and colour of the paper helped me to piece together the separate pages of the same letter, since she sometimes wrote the first page on one sort of paper and the second on another. However, an occasional letter survives in its envelope, the postmarks of these have given clues to their date, and the sequence of the story emerged as the pages were put together. All abbreviations have been extended and I have substituted my own punctuation for the odd dash which was all Cecilia used. Dates have been supplied wherever possible.

She had a beautiful clear script and I have enjoyed the jigsaw puzzle of editing these letters, not only for the companionship of her gay and intelligent mind but for the light thrown into a corner of the last century which illumines with humour and pathos the incidents of family life.

I am grateful to my daughter-in-law, Mrs. Nicholas Ridley, for her

PREFACE

help in selecting the most amusing and interesting passages from the letters, and to Mr. E. F. Collingwood for identifying so many of the people mentioned.

URSULA RIDLEY

Blagdon, 1958

CHAPTER ONE

Childhood

CECILIA was the eldest daughter of James Parke. Born in 1782, he was the ninth son and thirteenth child of Thomas Parke, a merchant of Liverpool. He was educated at Macclesfield Grammar School and Trinity College, Cambridge, where he had a brilliant career as a mathematician and classical scholar. In 1799 he won the Craven (University) Scholarship, and in the following year a Trinity scholarship. He won Sir William Browne's gold medal in 1802 with an alcaic ode, and was fifth wrangler and senior chancellor's medallist in classics the following year. He took the Member's Prize and was elected Fellow of his college in 1804 and proceeded M.A. in 1806.

He was called to the bar at the Inner Temple in 1813 and quickly acquired an extensive and lucrative common-law practice on the Northern Circuit and at Westminster. His most important case was when he appeared as junior counsel for the King against Queen Caroline in 1820. He continued to practise at the junior bar until 1828 when he was raised to the King's Bench and knighted. Here he remained until 1834 when he was made a Baron of the Court of Exchequer. From that time until his death in 1868 he occupied a unique position in the legal world and exercised a considerable influence on the law.

Greville said of him: "When Parke is present he rules the decisions of the court, which, by the way, he does with singular judgement and tact, by persuasion and suggestion and totally without arrogance and dictation—so unlike Brougham in every respect."

Lord Justice Denning[1] says that before the advent of Parke the

[1] *The Influence of Religion on Law*, Earl Grey Memorial lecture, delivered by Lord Justice Denning at King's College, Newcastle-upon-Tyne, 1953.

judges had interpreted the statutes "not only according to the language used but also so as to give 'force and life' to the intention of the legislature. But in the nineteenth century that broad view was supplanted by a rule which Baron Parke described as a golden rule. He said that statutes, and indeed all documents, were to be interpreted according to the grammatical and ordinary sense of the words. Even if the grammatical meaning gave rise to unjust results which Parliament never intended, nevertheless the grammatical rule must prevail."

It was this "golden rule," no doubt, that inspired Parke, as legal assessor in the trial of Lord Cardigan in 1841, to advise the House of Lords to acquit him on the grounds that the witnesses had not proved that Captain Harvey Garnet Phipps Tucket was the man who fought a duel with Lord Cardigan, since he was only mentioned in the indictment as Captain Harvey Tucket.

For this exactitude Parke is still remembered. His biographer in the *Dictionary of National Biography* says that he was neither

a great advocate nor a particularly skilful cross examiner, but he had a singular knack of rivetting the attention and winning the confidence of juries. His knowledge of the common law was profound and his mastery of detail consummate. His judgements, models of lucid statement and cogent reasoning, were always prepared with great care and usually committed to writing. [On being asked at some dinner party whether he had ever written a book, he replied, "No, Madam, my works are to be found in the pages of Meeson and Welsby."] His fault was an almost superstitious reverence for the dark technicalities of special pleading, and the reforms introduced by the Common-Law Procedure Acts of 1854 and 1855 occasioned his resignation from the Court of Exchequer.

The following year he was raised to the peerage and chose the title of Wensleydale from a property which he owned in the Yorkshire valley of that name. The patent had at first been drawn so as to confer on him a life peerage, but an attack of the gout prevented him from taking his seat on the day he should have done. The postponement gave their Lordships time to reflect and they referred the matter

BARON PARKE

to their Committee of Privileges. The Committee decided that the Crown had lost by disuse the power of creating a peerage with such a limitation—a decision of great constitutional significance.

A peerage in tail male was substituted, but as his three sons had all died in infancy the title became extinct when he died, although when his grandson, Sir Matthew White Ridley, fifth baronet, was created Viscount Ridley in 1900 he took as his second title that of Baron Wensleydale.

Parke married in 1817 Cecilia Arabella Frances, youngest daughter of Samuel Barlow of Middlethorpe Hall, Yorkshire, by whom he had six children. Lady Parke was gentle and wise, although she was extremely worldly in her choice of husbands for her daughters. Her grandson, Lord Ullswater, wrote of her in his autobiography: "There never was a more amiable or sweeter dispositioned old lady, to whom contradiction and contention were anathema." Their marriage was very happy and on the occasions when they had to be separated, usually when the Baron was on circuit, they wrote to each other every day. The Baron often wrote in court while learned counsel were making long addresses to the jury. No doubt they thought he was making careful notes of all they said, and the awe and even fear that he inspired in them might have been ameliorated, if they could have seen the tender, loving letters he was writing to his "beloved wife." Most of their early married life was spent in London, first in a house in Gower Street and later at 56 Park Street.

Cecilia Anne was born on 12 November 1819. Mary was a year younger. The three boys came next, and Alice, the only one to survive her parents, was born in 1829 and died in 1908.

The children were brought up in an atmosphere of great love and happiness. All Cecilia's letters and journals were carefully preserved and she expressed herself easily and fluently from the age of nine, when she wrote a prayer asking God to "let me get to sleep in a minute very comfortable and wake not later than half-past six." At eleven her tidy copperplate writing was already revealing a talent for describing the daily incidents of schoolroom life. Writing from Bootham, York, where the children were staying with their maternal grandmother Mrs. Barlow, she tells her "dearest little Mimmy" that "we do everything you told us to do as much as possible just as if you were looking at us all. Perhaps if you were here you would make us do more lessons than we do now, but Adèle is so afraid you should not find us in perfect health that she will not do so and she only wishes us to employ our playtime usefully." Adèle was the French governess, who was "very kind and good humoured and sends you *'beaucoup de choses de sa part'* and wants you back very much."

There is a charming description of Cecilia and Mary about this time written by Sydney Smith's daughter and biographer Saba, afterwards Lady Holland. Baron Parke was an old friend of Sydney Smith's, and Lady Holland records that "on one occasion hearing that Baron Parke and his family were unexpectedly detained in York by the dangerous illness of a relation whilst his two little girls were pining for country air after the whooping cough which they had just had, my father insisted that they should be sent to Foston to be under my mother's care. This of course made us a little anxious as my father had never had the complaint and I believe that it is often more severe with adults. The rule therefore was made that the dear little girls should never approach him nearer than arm and stick length, and I can see him even now laughing by fencing them off, or running away from them in the garden to their great delight, and their bright joyous little faces holding conference with him at the end of his stick. No evil ensued and the visit only served to cement closer a friendship of many years' standing."

In 1835, when Cecilia was fifteen, she began to keep a journal. It is not nearly so amusingly written as her letters, but it gives a good description of her education. All three sisters were extremely well educated and accomplished. Governesses at home, reading aloud and the opportunity of listening to the intelligent conversation of grown-up people were advantages that are lacking in the modern system of sending girls to boarding schools with little, if any, entertaining at home.

In addition to the routine background of lessons, Cecilia spoke fluent French, German and Italian and also learnt a little Spanish and Anglo-Saxon, while her father taught her Latin himself. Her formal education was supplemented by visits to the Royal Institution

CECILIA AND MARY

in Albemarle Street for the popular "Friday Lectures." Here she heard Faraday[1] give a "beautiful lecture on vibrations" which "lasted an hour and seemed very short," and another on "magnetism in minerals". Both are described in great detail.

Visits to Westminster Abbey and to see Barry's[2] designs for the new Houses of Parliament, accompanied by Frederick Mackenzie,[3] stimulated an interest in Gothic architecture, and she had painting lessons from Peter De Wint.[4] They all got a great deal of pleasure from sketching, and Mary in particular had real talent. Many of her water-colour landscapes are in the possession of her great-great niece Winifred Nicholson, but unfortunately none of Cecilia's has survived. De Wint may have been a good teacher but they did not care much for him and Cecilia refers to him as "stingy old De Wint whose domineering thought is I am sure *money*, for we have never had a lesson from him in which he did not contrive to talk about it." But he talked of other things too and regaled them with scraps of information about his fellow-painters. "Fuseli drew best under the influence of toasted cheese" and "Turner is completely mad which De Wint says is owing to drinking." "Titian's first attempt was a virgin which he coloured with the juice of flowers."

The Royal Academy exhibitions, which were then held at Somerset House, were regularly attended and freely criticised. Landseer was Cecilia's favourite painter and on visiting his studio she wrote: "We were kept waiting exactly one hour and then admitted to see three of the most beautiful things possible. One is a portrait of Lord Ossulston[5]." The Parkes were evidently on calling terms with other

[1] Michael Faraday (1791–1867) was at this time at the height of his career. As a lecturer to children he was said to have been at his best and most lucid.

[2] Sir Charles Barry (1795–1860) won the competition to rebuild the new Houses of Parliament on 29 February 1836.

[3] Topographical draughtsman (1788–1860).

[4] Landscape painter in water-colour (1748–1849).

[5] Lord Ossulston (1810–99) was the eldest son of the fifth Earl of Tankerville, of Chillingham, Northumberland. M.P. for North Northumberland 1832–59, when he succeeded his father. Married in 1850 Lady Olivia Montagu.

C.R.—B

painters, for another entry in Cecilia's journal records: "I went with Mama to call on Sir Augustus Callcott,[1] and whilst we were there a little funny looking man came in and talked very amusingly with a tiny voice and a very broad Scotch accent and to my great surprise I found afterwards that this personage was Campbell the poet.[2] He gave a funny account of having once been obliged to spend a day at Rouen, which he found so dull that he paid a visit to the doctor of the town and gave him a fee of 2/6 an hour for talking to him."

Music also played an important part in their education. In addition to playing the piano and the harp Cecilia had singing lessons from Scappa, "who was not particularly complimentary but pronounced that I shall sing some day or other". Concerts and the Opera were frequently attended: "We went to a concert for the relief of Decayed Musicians" when "Grisi[3] sang beautifully . . . and Madame Filipowicz played the violin which looked excessively funny and made us laugh very much." On another occasion she heard Garcia[4] "who had a fine voice and a frightful face."

Outdoor activities included archery lessons and daily rides, either in the Park or "with Papa down to Westminster. I rode Papa's *Blacky* which is very tremendous but quite gentle and nice and such a trotter —we beat all the law at trotting without a doubt. It does one a great deal of good to get these morning rides and then we have the advantage of having all the day before us for business."

On 4 February 1836 she wrote:

We went to the House of Lords to hear the King's speech at the opening of Parliament. Lord Cottenham took his seat, Lord Denman and all the Judges, Lord Devon, Lord Goodrich, Lord Melbourne, Lord Lansdowne, the Archbishops of York and Canterbury, Noun Effendi and all the foreign ambassadors etc. were there. The King

[1] Landscape painter (1799–1844). Knighted 1837. His wife, Maria Dundas, wrote *Little Arthur's History of England.*

[2] Thomas Campbell (1777–1844) was living in London at this time.

[3] Famous soprano (1811–69), much admired by Greville.

[4] Pauline Garcia (1821–1910), a "girl with a miraculous voice", was a friend of George Sand and the heroine of her novel *Consuelo.* She is better known by her married name of Madame Viardot.

had his splendid crown on and looked very old and decrepit. He could not read his speech, and after bungling and asking Lord Melbourne every word he at length asked for a candle; upon which one wax one and one tallow were produced, and he addressed the Lords and gentlemen of the House of Commons in a little extempore harangue to tell them that he had been prevented reading properly from want of light and would begin again; which he did and read it pretty well the second time. He mentioned his offer of mediation between France and the United States etc. After his departure Lord Langdale took his place which was a very pretty ceremony; he took the oaths, was then led to the junior Baron's seat and returned to shake hands with the Chancellor.

[Another amusing anecdote of William IV that Baron Parke heard from Lord Brougham was that he "once fell asleep on a sopha by the Duchess of Buccleuch and fancying that he was in bed called out half-awake: 'Ma'am I have got both my feet thro' a hole in the sheet.'" In fact, Cecilia's journals are full of little bits of gossip: "The Duchess of Sutherland has bought four dozen pocket handkerchiefs at £25 a piece." And "when Lady Davy was staying in Italy all her stories began 'Quando io son stato at Dunrobino.'"[1] Or "Lady Haddington is said to have all the qualities of a poker except its warmth."

Cecilia also had a taste for curious pieces of information, sometimes scientific, sometimes merely odd. "I never knew before that in one frosty night rabbits will grow quite fat and that they become thin as suddenly." "2 cwt. of conger eels are consumed in London every day." "A sailor's life is much shorter than a soldier's—probably owing to the early age at which people are sent out to sea." "The new brigand looking hats that the common people wear are called *Wide Awakes* because there is no *nap* on them."

In March 1836 Cecilia was confirmed in the Chapel Royal by the Bishop of London. The experience moved her to a new and greater

[1] Lady Davy, widow of Sir Humphrey Davy, inventor of the Davy Safety Lamp for miners, was a prominent figure in Rome and London society. Dunrobino is "Italian" for Dunrobin, belonging to the Duke of Sutherland.

awareness of moral issues and religious precepts. Her longing to be good, accompanied by a sense of failure and guilt, is common enough in adolescence; Cecilia's introspective entries in her journal are only exceptional for the honesty of her heart-searching:]

2 April 1836   *London*

I felt more than ever today how weak my best resolutions are and how totally ineffectual. I felt often again today a sort of jealousy rising in my mind—a jealousy even of Mary, my own sister (is it possible?)—and I could not crush this in any way but by retiring for a few minutes to pray for strength and support, to enable me to love my sisters and all people with an affection pure from selfishness and full of charity.

7 April 1836

Oh what a weak creature I am! What a mean vanity is firmly seated in my heart. We went to a dance and it was very pleasant, but I do not think I could go out every night to balls and parties without being too much occupied and engrossed by that sort of thing. However I hope to gain gradually more strength and firmness of principle to enable me to raise myself above all the things of this world.

[And she completed the last page of her journal with this self-analysis:]

16 May 1836

How often do I find that I have made others uncomfortable by not doing my best to please them, how often have I neglected opportunities of giving pleasure, have I been cross and ill tempered for no reason, and then felt a sort of stubbornness and pride which prevented me making amends for it. If I look over my past life, I find that this has continuously been the case with my sisters, with Mama and Papa, with Di, with Mrs. Juffs and many other people, and I know that this fault is the one which is most disagreeable to all those who are near me. It is difficult to conquer it, as most often the hasty words come out before I am aware of it, and therefore I must firmly resolve never to say anything without reflecting whether or not it will give pain to anybody . . . My education and circumstances are such, that I cannot be guilty of any flagrant sin, but so much the more must I govern my most secret thoughts and inclinations, for unto whom much is given from him will much be required . . . I find in my heart a great disposition to that horrible vice jealousy—I am determined through the grace of God to conquer it, however deeply rooted it may be . . . Whenever I feel the least inclination to be uncomfortable on hearing others praised or admired I will always put myself in their place, identify myself with them and rejoice that they are pleased . . . There is another fault which is continually rising up within me—it is vanity, a sort of desire to be admired or praised, to be thought good looking or clever or amiable, which I am afraid has often more power than the desire of being so really. When I reflect upon this, it is certainly a most ridiculous idea . . . for when I look into my own heart I see plainly how very little reason I can ever have to be vain, and find, on the contrary, the greatest reason to be very humble. But when I am in the midst of society at some ball or party, I always find myself with a secret wish to draw attention upon me, and this is so deeply rooted that it is very difficult to conquer, but yet I am now about to promise solemnly before God that I will renounce the "world the flesh and the devil" and it must therefore be my most earnest endeavour to fulfil this.

[Fortunately Cecilia did not succeed in renouncing the world. Instead it was the journal, with all its pious, impossible resolutions which was put aside—for the next three years at any rate.]

CHAPTER TWO

The London Season

CECILIA came out in 1837 at the age of seventeen. In the spring her parents took her and Mary abroad, to Switzerland, Austria and Hungary where they stayed with Prince Esterhazy.[1] They returned through Paris where they bought her "coming out" trousseau. On their return to London she wrote several letters to Miss Fanny Barlow, Lady Parke's eldest unmarried sister, who lived at Bootham with old Mrs. Barlow.

May 1837   *56 Park St. London*

Dearest Aunt Fanny, . . . We are still very occupied in tidying the house, which in the meantime is rather in a state of confusion, for we find it difficult to make our old closets and drawers contain our wardrobe with its Paris additions, which are not to be despised. I wish you could have seen our carriage packed for leaving that city of dressmakers and milliners—a pile of three large cases behind, a basket imperial on the top and a Dutch oven hanging underneath, which last article was used so often as a footstool by the little boys who climbed the carriage that it was several times in danger of being left on the road. However, by good fortune we not only arrived safe but escaped paying any duty whatever for our purchases, although every single thing was unpacked and examined in London. And now that the fear of a customs house is no longer before our eyes we are full of grief and sorrow that we did not buy more. Paris is wonderfully improved as to public buildings and convenient footways in the streets, and the inhabitants have all an air of business and "reflection" which is no doubt all the better for them; but at the same time they have

[1] Austrian Ambassador at London 1815–42.

lost all their smartness, the art of cookery is visibly declining and the shopkeepers are an exceedingly impertinent, disagreeable set of people. The Opera was beautiful and as Lady Granville[1] lent us her box we enjoyed it to perfection. But the thing now *à la mode* is a Vaudeville called *Toulouson*—as nonsensical as its name which means nothing at all . . .

You would be surprised if you saw Mary and me now, for we have got some new French stays and are become such wonderful shapes that every time I see myself in the glass I open the *eyes of astonishment* and lift up the voice of *admiration*. We are also *bejacketted* in a very tight fitting style and altogether our appearance is very wondrous to behold . . . Aunt Fitzroy[2] drank tea with us the other day and excited our indignation by telling us we made our hair look like a Methodist Parson's wig. Goodbye, dearest Aunt Fanny, pray give my love to Grandmama,

Your very affectionate niece,
Cecilia Parke.

May 1837   *London*

Dearest Aunt Fanny, . . . The rest Mama expected to find at home is of a very fatiguing nature, for she has been out nearly every evening since her return and often to 3 or 4 parties on the same day, so that she finds it rather inconvenient not having all her gowns, turbans etc. and is obliged to be dressed nearly the same every evening which will soon give rise to the epithet "Lady Parke with her eternal green velvet." I hope you who are so fashionable a person have already made all your sleeves quite tight to your arm—but the question is useless for I know you would not think of going out with such an old fashioned thing as a full sleeve at present, particularly when you hear that Lady Goodrich has asked for a pattern for one of these curtailed wings . . .

Sometimes Mama sends Mary and me out in the carriage and we go to street after street knocking at about every third door and dropping

---

[1] The first Earl of Granville was Ambassador at Paris 1830–41.

[2] Mrs. Fitzroy was Lady Parke's elder sister. She married Charles Fitzroy, second son of the first Lord Southampton, in 1816.

cards. I always feel an awful responsibility as to directing our course without going any roundabout ways, so that I hope at least this charming employment will teach me the map of London and fit me for a coachman's place in case of need . . . In the course of shopping at Waterloo House we heard that all the *Challis*[1] are now made in England and exported to Paris instead of being imported—they are made at Norwich and printed in Scotland—the patterns being all designed from nature by a Sussex farmer who receives £1400 a year.

June 1837   *London*

My dear Aunt Fanny . . . The death of the poor old King[2] has put an end to all balls for the present, but I hear they will begin again directly after the funeral—indeed the Opera is not put off at all, which I think is very disrespectful to royalty. Prince Esterhazy's was the last I went to, and the hottest and the latest, for Mama broke through her rule of never being last in favour of a good partner, and we staid till $\frac{1}{2}$ past 4 when the birds were all singing and the sun shining and making us feel quite ashamed of our dissipation. The young Queen seems to have begun her reign in the most promising way. Papa was delighted with her delivery of her first speech, which she made to the Privy Councillors immediately after the death of the King, and with her way of executing the business and issuing the orders, which she did just as if she had been long accustomed to it, although she had only been told the same morning of all she would have to do. She behaved with the greatest dignity and walked out of the room with the most queenlike step she could assume—but as soon as she thought herself out of sight she skipped off to her mother as nimbly as possible, which was betrayed to all the gentlemen by a large looking-glass she had not thought of.

Goodbye, Dearest Aunt F. Your very affectionate niece

Cecilia Parke.

---

[1] Challis: a soft woollen material with a small design, either of dots or sprigs of flowers. Still used extensively in the Southern States of America.

[2] William IV died on 20 June 1837.

[In 1839 Cecilia started to keep a journal again. "I think I cannot begin a new book better than with good resolutions, and therefore I determine to follow the counsel of the old divine and not to allow 'swallows to build nests in my hair,' besides which I intend this book to be very tidily kept and neatly written—and above all never to be polluted by the eyes of Evans [presumably a housemaid]."

The whole of the spring and summer was spent in a continual round of social engagements:]

Yesterday we dined at Lord de Grey's[1] and had 22 people, many of whom came in in the middle of dinner, for his Lordship never waits a second for a single living creature. . . . After the feast we went to a party at the Duchess of Roxburghe's where every snob in London was present. The poor Duchess is quite overwhelmed with her acquaintance and I really believe she will die of good nature.

We went for a few minutes to an unknown lady called Mrs. Douglas Holford, who had a nasty party of such ugly people that Mama declared they were all masked, and a house like a mouse trap at the door of which she stood so that we could not escape.

We went to Lady Domville's[2]—the nicest ball I have been at this year. I danced with Lord Loftus[3] who had been eating onions and a charming Mr. Taylor whom I thought *superlative*. He never talks of people but always *mortals* or *beings*. 33 people asked me to dance.

[Another night at dinner, she sat next to Sir Edward Bulwer Lytton]

who disgusted me extremely—he was very affected and asked me if I should like to be an Opera dancer. He seems to have no truth in him—he is all distorted and out of drawing—not his body but his mind. We afterwards went to a tail[4] where we saw a collection of

---

[1] First Earl de Grey of Wrest in Bedfordshire, married in 1805 the youngest daughter of the first Earl of Enniskillen.

[2] Maria, daughter of Isaac Solly, married in 1807 Sir William Domville, second Baronet.

[3] Lord Loftus succeeded his father as third Marquis of Ely in 1845.

[4] An evening party.

unwashed uncombed philosophers and among them Judge Haliburton the author of *Sam Slick*.[1]

We went to Lord Brougham's[2] great party to see the Russian Prince who is nice looking.[3] It was an interesting assembly of great men and pretty ladies. Lady B. received the company reclining on a couch in an attitude copied from Venus with the addition of a smelling bottle.

[Once a week she went to Almack's, the famous club or Assembly Room, where for a ten-guinea subscription a series of twelve weekly balls was given. Admission was extremely difficult and much sought after by ambitious mothers. "We went to Almack's which was splendid—quite a beautiful sight. I danced all the time and enjoyed myself although Mama abused all my partners."

She not only danced all night and most nights, but she burnt the candle at both ends:]

Chief Justice Tindal's[4] breakfast—it was quite delightful—we came home at ½ past 10 and had plenty of dancing and walking about.

[And a few weeks later she writes:]

I got up at an early hour and under Mr. Sydney Smith's[5] care we

---

[1] Thomas Chandler Haliburton (1796–1865) was a judge in Nova Scotia. Writing a series of volumes under the pseudonym Sam Slick, he told his countrymen many home truths, which made him far more popular outside Nova Scotia than in it.

[2] Lord Brougham married in 1819 Mary Anne, widow of John Spalding. He was no longer Lord Chancellor at the time of this party.

[3] The Grand Duke Alexander (later Czar Alexander II) paid a state visit to Queen Victoria in May 1839.

[4] Sir Nicholas Conyngham Tindal (1776–1846) was at Trinity College, Cambridge, with Sir James Parke. M.P. for Wigtown Burghs, 1824, and for Harwich, 1826. Solicitor General, 1826. Chief Justice of Common Pleas from 1829.

[5] Sydney Smith (1771–1845) was at this time Canon of St Paul's and was living at 56 Green Street, London.

went to breakfast with Mr. Rogers.[1] The company consisted of Miss
Rogers, Mr. Milnes,[2] O'Brien[3] and to my great dismay Mr. Colvile.
They were all so agreeable and so funny that I was quite fatigued
with laughing. I never saw Mr. Sydney so delightfully amusing and
particularly about a trip to America in company with Mr. Rogers.
He said they should go into the back settlements and each marry a
squaw, then Mr. Rogers must make an addition to the pleasures of
memory on the delights of *Squawism*. If they quizzed the Americans
he said they should be tarred and feathered and, lovely as they both
were, that would be very trying . . . An American wishing to
describe a well bred man said 'he was quite at home on a carpet.' . . .
Mr. Sydney, asked what was the meanest equipage he could employ,
said he thought in emergency he might bestride his curate. But his
jokes do not bear repeating—they depend so much on his countenance
and manner.

[James Colvile, whose presence at this breakfast party caused Cecilia
so much dismay, was an ardent admirer. He was a great friend
of Richard Monckton Milnes, with whom he had been at Trinity,
Cambridge, where he was an honours graduate in mathematics.
He was a promising barrister and was later elected a Fellow of the
Royal Society and knighted in 1848 for his services as Advocate
General to the East India Company in Calcutta, becoming a judge
on his return to England. Cecilia met him in February 1839 at a
party given by Lady Minto and thought him "very very nice. I felt
my sensible resolutions were weak as water," she added. A few weeks
later at "another delightful party everybody was very agreeable
and more particularly Mr. Colvile. I should have enjoyed myself

[1] Samuel Rogers (1763–1855), the poet, lived in a house he had built
himself in St James's Place, where he was renowned for the "exquisite
taste, artistic and social which distinguished both his house and the company he gathered around him". His sister acted as hostess for him.

[2] Richard Monckton Milnes (1809–85), friend of Florence Nightingale,
was at this time M.P. for Pontefract. He was created first Lord
Houghton in 1863.

[3] Either William O'Brien (1803–64), Irish Nationalist, or his brother
Edward (1808–40), who was an author.

excessively if I had not felt I was foolish, and when we came home I spent an hour talking or rather listening to Mama who certainly is right. I must not give way entirely to my inclinations—it would be worse than silly—but if it cannot be, I wish I did not see him so often, as all my wisdom vanishes when I do." But less than a week after Mama's warning "Mr. Colvile called and was more agreeable than I have ever seen him and the more I think of him the more I like him." A few days later he called again: "From his manner I am convinced he means something and I am wretched at the thought of it, for I am sure I have behaved foolishly."

At the beginning of March she was removed from temptation and taken to York for the festivities of the Assizes. Here she quickly found distraction in the attentions of Mr. Harry Thompson, another Trinity graduate with honours in mathematics who became Liberal M.P. for Whitby and was created Sir Harry Meysey Thompson, Bart., in 1847. The day after Cecilia met him at a ball she was "surprised while having a solitary sit with Aunt Fanny by receiving a lovely bouquet said to be brought by a gentleman smoking a cigar and nameless." The next day the nameless "hero" turned out to be Mr. Thompson, "who Aunt Fanny has christened '*Pike*' and whom I do *like*." Throughout the month she spent at York he was an assiduous escort and dancing partner, though she was not allowed entirely to forget Mr. Colvile, for on 26 March "Mama had a letter from Aunt Fitzroy full of unpleasant gossip about me and Mr. Colvile. I certainly am not in love," she comments, "and I fear I never shall be."

On her return to London in April Mr. Thompson followed her and "had an interview with Mama which ended as we expected." Next day "Mama showed me a letter from H. T. full of feeling. I was very much astonished and distressed. I did not think he would have felt it." A week later she wrote "We are very much troubled about Mr. H. T. Mrs. Childers is still trying to bring it on but I feel that it is wiser not, for I really do not know enough of him." On the night of 6 May the Parkes gave a ball at Park Street and next day Cecilia confided to her journal: "I was perfectly happy until I saw Mr. T. looking so wretched that it went to my heart. I began to think: am I right in making him unhappy? but I believe really I am." It was not until 2 July, however, that she put an end to it all. "Harry came and I was obliged to have an interview with him. I'm glad it's all over both for his sake and mine, as I am sure I could never have loved him enough. It must have been a very disagreeable season for him."

Next day she ran into Mr. Colvile again at the Opera—"the only nice being there who only served to make me uncomfortable. Oh how I wish people did not want for money," she added wistfully, which makes one think that Mama was at the bottom of all her indecision.

But other beaux were waiting to console her. Mr. Forbes had been very sentimental all the summer, saying "such pretty things" and "singing with exquisite feeling". On 22 July "Mama told me that Mr. Forbes had actually proposed to her for me. I was thunderstruck." And Granville Vernon Harcourt, sixth son of the Archbishop of York, whom Lady Parke could not possibly have approved of, was another favourite whom she told Aunt Fanny "deserves so much praise that I will not undertake it." She summed up this gay if troubled season in the following letter to Aunt Fanny:]

29 July 1839   *56 Park St.*

Thank you, dear Aunt, for your advice and hint. You were right in thinking it could trouble me much. I really am torn in two and do nothing but curse the misery of having such a nasty trumpery undirected character as mine. It is so tiresome that one can have no previous experience in marrying, for that is the only way I have in making up my mind. But I am at least decided in being your affectionate niece and I shall just ease my mind by telling you all we have been about. We have been enjoying ourselves excessively and I do not think I have ever had a happier time than last month— since Mr. Thompson disappeared, and with him all doubt, anxiety and bother. We have had quantities of little parties—all charming— but by far the most memorable that ever has been or will be was one last Thursday at which Lord Holland and his Lady[1] were present. I

---

[1] Lady Holland, the great Whig hostess of Holland House, was sixty-nine at the time of this dinner-party. Lord Holland was three years younger.

do not know if you have ever seen her, but if not picture to yourself a tall and stately old lady, very erect but very fat with a stern face and a gruff voice and great remains of beauty. Lord Lansdowne[1] and Mr. Rutherford[2] were detained at the House and Lady Holland being hungry we sat down to dinner minus Mr. Greville and Mr. Austin[3] who came in later. Mrs. Beaumont,[4] Mr. John Ashley[5] and Mr. Webster (the American)[6] were the rest of the party and there was a great deal of interesting conversation carried on by Lord Holland who is very playful and charming and Mr. Webster who is full of information which he gives in fine slow clear language. At dinner Lady H. sat between Mr. W. and Mr. Ashley and made herself very remarkable by the quantity she ate and said—amongst other things she asked Mr. W. how old he was and on his saying 56 she exclaimed "That is not true—look at the brilliancy of your eyes— the brightness of your complexion—I never saw eyes with such a lustre before." At which Mr. W. seemed rather amused and looked unaccustomed to such compliments. Lord H. was obliged to go off early to the House and soon afterwards Her Ladyship's carriage was announced containing her doctor Allen,[7] who, knowing that nothing would persuade her to go back to South Street alone, had come to escort her. Unfortunately she did not feel inclined to go and tried all means of persuading Dr. A. to get out or to wait, but it was all in vain and to our great relief the old lady took her departure, leaving us all full of

[1] Third Marquess of Lansdowne, Lord President of the Council 1830–41.

[2] Andrew Rutherford, Lord Advocate and M.P. for Leith Burghs in 1839.

[3] Charles Austin (1799–1874) was said to be the most brilliant lawyer of his day and regarded as a rival to Macaulay in conversational power.

[4] Mrs. Beaumont, or Madame Beaumont as she was universally called, was the illegitimate daughter and heiress of Sir Thomas Blackett, Bart., of Bretton in Yorkshire. She married Colonel Beaumont, M.P.

[5] John Ashley Cooper, M.P. (1808–67), fourth son of the sixth Earl of Shaftesbury.

[6] Daniel Webster (1782–1852), American lawyer, statesman and orator, was on a visit to London in 1839.

[7] Dr. Allen lived permanently with Lord and Lady Holland as a sort of companion to them both.

horrors at her and wishing sincerely she might never again enter the house. Mr. Webster is a very striking man and talks in the most interesting way but very slow. His lady friends are drawly and vulgar looking.

Goodbye, dearest Aunt F. Give a kiss to Grandmamma for me and believe me your very affectionate niece

Cecilia Parke.

CHAPTER THREE

Ampthill

IN 1837 Baron Parke had rented a lease of Ampthill Park from the Duke of Bedford. It is a place of some historic interest, as Katharine of Aragon lived there for two years while her divorce was proceeding. The site of the old castle where she lived is marked by a stone cross with an inscription written by Horace Walpole, friend of the Earl of Upper Ossory who owned it at one time. The house which the Parkes lived in was built in 1694 by Lord Ashburnham to the design of a Captain Winde, though Hawksmoor is also said to have had a hand in it and it was later remodelled by Sir William Chambers. Today it is in a sad state of repair and is being used as a sanatorium by Group Captain Cheshire.

It is in very beautiful country with a wooded park overlooking the plain of Bedford towards the Chiltern Hills. Here the Baron and Lady Parke entertained a large number of friends, all of them well known in legal, literary and political circles. Although they had rented the property in 1837 it was not until 1839 that they first went to stay there, and, as Cecilia records in her journal, "settled the weighty matter of our rooms to our mutual satisfaction." She was soon writing to Miss Barlow to describe it:

September 1839   *Ampthill*

Dearest Aunt Fanny, For the first time since we have been in the country there is a possibility of a frank, as Aunt Fitzroy is going into a land flowing with honourable members and right honourable Lords and will no doubt take charge of a letter to thank you for your delightfully long epistle which was really so undeserved that it filled me with shame. You are right in supposing that the repose of Ampthill is

AMPTHILL PARK

good both for body and mind after the long spell we had had of London and its gaieties, and it is certainly a most pleasing way of recovering one's senses. The place is perfect in every respect and the more we see of it the more beauties we discover in it. There are subjects without end for sketching and we have not been altogether idle in that way, although we now and then are exceedingly angry with ourselves for not doing better and are obliged to admire each other's drawings to keep up our spirits. The people about here are extremely prim and decorous and I am sadly afraid they will look upon us as Goths and Vandals and think us hardly fit for decent society when they see Mary and me trudge out, laden with books, shawls and three-legged stools "in search of the picturesque."

Lord and Lady de Grey are now at Wrest and we went over there the other day to see the new house, which is beautiful and entirely Lord de Grey's own planning. He draws the patterns for all the ceilings and ornaments of every description and then overlooks the execution of all his orders, so that he must look upon it all as his child —and a most promising one it is. Another nice person we have made acquaintance with is Mr. Harvey[1], a young gentleman who possesses a nice old place 12 miles off and lives there with his mother and sisters in the most comfortable style, which we can answer for, as we went there last Monday to lunch. It was a long way and we lost our way as usual and arrived as hungry as hunters. After we had partaken of an excellent repast we went to Warden which is a show place belonging to Lord Ongley and close to Mr. Harvey's, and there we saw the most extraordinary garden in the world made out of a bog; full of little old summer houses on little round hills, china vases, busts, coloured lamps—in short quite a fairyland but more of a Chinese fairy than a European one . . . Good bye, dearest Aunt F.

[Other near neighbours were the Samuel Whitbreads of Southill (he was known as the Chevalier de Malte) and Lord and Lady[2]

---

[1] John Harvey of Ickwell, Bedfordshire.

[2] Lord Tavistock (1788–1861), eldest son of the sixth Duke of Bedford. He sat in the House of Lords, at the time Cecilia knew him, in his father's Barony of Howland. Lady Tavistock was the eldest daughter of

Tavistock at Oakley, where Cecilia spent a couple of days in
October:]

It is a very gay foreign-looking summer place and when we arrived
there Lady Tavistock came sailing out of her veranda in white and
lilies of the valley and conducted us into a beautiful little fairy
luncheon room, so that I really almost fancied it a dream until I had
satisfied myself of the reality of some chicken pie on the table. Lord T.
is kindness and goodness itself and Lady T. as amiable as possible.
But O her dress last night was so funny—brown crape trimmed with
gold quite in unity with Alpheus. However she has great taste in
everything but her dress and has the prettiest collection of songs and
teapots I ever saw.

[It was not long before Cecilia found as many beaux and suitors in
Bedfordshire as she had in London. Staying at Woburn Abbey in
September she met Count Thun: [1] "I have never been in such high
spirits as these last three days—all owing to that nice dear Count",
Cecilia wrote in her journal on 30 September, and "when shall we
see him again?" she wonders. She did not have to wait long, for on
18 October she wrote to Aunt Fanny:]

Dearest of Aunts, We expect two frankers in a few days to my great
joy, as I am just now seized with a great desire to write, a violent
passion for universal correspondence, and more particularly an
especial inclination to write to you, which is nursed and fostered into
life by a rainy morning. From this I fear you will expect that I have
something interesting to say, but the truth is that all I have to tell
you is that we are as happy as it is possible for human beings to be
and that I do not know why or wherefore. I feel more gay and happy,
—more full of joy and peace this autumn than I ever did before. Yet

the third Earl of Harrington and was a Lady of the Bedchamber
1837–41.

[1] Count Joseph Mathias and his elder brother Prince Thun did the
Grand Tour from 1830 till 1840. His descendant describes him as a
mangeur de cœurs.

notwithstanding this I am rather in a contemplative melancholy mood this morning and I will tell you why. Last night after dinner when we were sitting thinking of nothing we heard rather an unusual sound breaking in upon the stillness of the hall—the door opened, and we beheld Count Thun whom I had imagined to be just embarked for Germany and tossing about in some horrible steamer. It was like an apparition and yet it was a reality—there stood the dear Count and right glad we all were to see him. He had come all the way from London to bid us farewell and was obliged to go away at 5 this morning and leave England today. Now can you imagine any words in which to express our feelings at such a charming romantic conduct. Is it not really quite touching, perfectly irresistible and worthy of being sung in immortal lays by an angel or a Shakespeare—or a *Milnes*? But alas I am no poet—mine is not the pen of a ready writer, so all I can possibly do is to think about it, which I am sure we shall all do, for who could ever forget it? He sang all his nice "*schwärmerische Lieder*" and we had a charming delightful evening together and a very tender parting, not without a hope that the dear Count may return next autumn to enliven and enchant us.

[But the Count never returned, and Mr. Harvey of Ickwell soon absorbed Cecilia's attention. She went to stay with him for a party where "Mrs. Littledale sang nicely and we had a supper of oysters and substantials and so ended the evening merrily, merrily." Next day "Mr. Harvey lionised us over his house and grounds and showed us his old keeper. I am all astonishment about him. I expected he would be devoted to Mary, and behold instead of that he is full of tenderness and affection to me and looks so sad and sighs so that I feel quite melancholy." Two days later she wrote: "A dreadful melancholy day—snow out of doors and trouble within. The party from Ickwell came and went on to Woburn. Mr. H. stayed here and proposed. I was beyond measure surprised and distressed and felt very unhappy all the evening. I feel I have been wrong in walking so much with him. I am in despair about it."

Her despair was short-lived, however, and in January 1840 she wrote to Aunt Fanny:]

We had a very merry Christmas, the merriest we ever had—
the trees all dressed in rime and looking more lovely than anything
I ever saw except in my imagination of some enchanted country.
However, much as I enjoyed it, I must confess that it was cold and
that poor dear Ampthill is the coldest of cold places, so that all chilly
beings like Moppy[1] and Aunt Fitzroy were no doubt uncomfortable
whilst hard creatures like myself were on the contrary extremely
happy and flourished amazingly amidst "winter yelling through
the troublous air." . . . Mr. Dundas[2] is much improved—far more
sociable than he was. He has mixed more with people in general
lately and rubbed off his angles which used to annoy one so much.
At Christmas he was good nature itself, which was proved by his sub-
mitting to have a wig pinned on by Alice and performing Milton for
our amusement. Mary looked very bright as Judith and behaved
very well, but I did not as St. Cecilia, for I laughed and had so much
rouge that I must have looked like Madame Vestris.[3] We were very
nearly having a grand scene one night—Mrs. Murchison[4] wore an
elegant hat with a weeping feather and she was retiring to rest with
her bed candle held gracefully in one hand and her fan turned pen-
sively the other way when there was a smell of fire. Mr. Dundas
clawed the sweet little hat from off her head, Mr. Duncombe[5]

[1] Mop or Moppy was Mary's nickname.

[2] Sir David Dundas (1799–1877), a Scottish lawyer and politician, was
a great friend of Baron Parke's and a constant visitor to Park Street and
Ampthill. He later used to stay at Blagdon when he went the Northern
Circuit. He wanted to marry Alice but remained a bachelor. Lord
Ullswater describes him (in *A Speaker's Commentary*) as having a "fine
presence, a handsome face, beetling eyebrows and a head of upstanding
grey hair."

[3] Lucia Elizabeth Vestris (1797–1856) was a well-known opera singer.
She married Charles Mathews and helped him in the management of
Covent Garden and the Lyceum. She is said to have been "unrivalled
as a stage singer."

[4] Roderick Impey Murchison (1792–1871), geologist and F.R.S.,
married in 1814 Charlotte, daughter of General Hugonin.

[5] Thomas Slingsby Duncombe, M.P., nephew of the first Lord
Feversham, and son of Thomas Duncombe of Copgrove, Yorks.

trampled it underfoot, and there stood Mrs. Murchison, her hair neatly dressed and luckily all her own, vowing eternal gratitude to her two deliverers. Her feather looked rather ill but that was all, for the hat escaped wonderfully. Mr. Murchison was pronounced by all parties to be vain and tiresome, and so he was until he was left alone when his merits became more apparent. He was a great contrast to the other people—all so very natural and straightforward . . .

Goodbye, dearest Aunt Fanny. Pray read *The Hour and the Man*.[1] The "hour" and the dinner is coming so I must end.

Your very affectionate niece
Cecilia Parke.

[The entries in her journal for the summer season of 1840 are more discreet than the year before and record only a series of social engagements and lists of people who dined or called without mentioning any more affairs of the heart. They returned to Ampthill for the late summer and autumn, and the two following letters are characteristic of the life they led:]

August 1840   *Wrest*

My dear Aunt Fanny, Here we are established for a day or two in a comfortable corner of this magnificent house and there is a little gap of time before luncheon which I mean to fill up by scribbling to you on her Ladyship's *young lady paper*—not superfine as you will observe. We came here yesterday. Lord and Lady Radstock,[2] Mr. Rogers and Mr. Luttrell[3] are the party . . . The two wits are disappointing. Mr. Luttrell ate too much and went to sleep all the evening, having no remains of wit except a sarcastic twitch of his nose. This morning he looks better but he has not yet unlocked his treasures. Mr. Rogers shines like a bright star in comparison, saying

[1] An historical romance by Harriet Martineau, published in 1840.

[2] Second Baron Radstock (1786–1857) served in the Royal Navy. He married in 1823 Esther Caroline, daughter of John Puget, a director of the Bank of England.

[3] Henry Luttrell (?1765–1835) was the illegitimate son of the second Earl of Carhampton. He was well known as a wit and a member of the Holland House circle.

sweet things and looking sour. I never saw him so entertaining as he has been in his quiet way. Lord de Grey is smiling and kind as always and I am happy to say he has not cut off his moustachios. I like to see them for they are thick with Yeomanry recollections. Lady de Grey looks astonishingly handsome and frisks about like a young lamb, but a very graceful and dignified lamb it must be. She is clad in white flowing muslin and she sits in a room of white satin and gold and china and miniatures. She talks a great deal and very well but it requires all her grace and sweetness to talk as she does without being disagreeable . . . There was much interesting conversation last night concerning war, chiefly kept up by the Countess and Mr. Rogers who says the Chinese mean to frighten the English by strange noises . . . What it is to be old and to have lived in troublous times!

Now I have described our party I will transfer you to Ampthill with its lovely shades, its ancient oaks, its scraggy chickens and their active little mistress. There could not well be a greater contrast than the two houses are, although Ampthill is not uncomfortable but this is so bright and new and dazzling that it overpowers all other lights.

November 1840   *Ampthill*

Mama is making a shift for a poor woman, sitting at a round table covered with books, bags and workboxes, a lamp and a flat candle. Alice is singing under the guidance of Louisa for our amusement· She has been afflicted with a pair of stays with bones which cause infinite trouble and dismay to the whole household. However she has had a gown made upon them which would astonish you. It is a Douglas plaid—tight waist, tight sleeves, a most wax-like fit and when she appears in the said gown she looks most awfully tall. Mary is reading and thinking by turns and I have just been making acquaintance with some new funguses and now am going to have a little chat with you.

We have spent a very quiet time indeed *this term* and not been out anywhere. Papa has read aloud to us every evening—generally some play with funny dialogue which we enjoy exceedingly. We draw without ceasing—Mary generally in the *head* line and I stand in a very

LADY PARKE

artist-like fashion at an easel and dash away at my landscapes . . .
As usual business thickens just before we go to town. It is very
difficult to settle what to take and what to leave behind. Then there
are shoals of little bills to pay at little shops at Ampthill, and above all
there is a great deal to say and do to the school, which we found rather
in a disorderly state when we came back. The mice wanted the cat
very much. There had been a rebellion against hair-cutting which
went so far that we were obliged to dismiss the ringleader who was
a tall girl with a hideous thick yellow wig of which she seemed
particularly fond. Now that she is gone the rest are rather awestruck
and give up their heads to the executioner without even a sigh.

There has been a great deal of illness in the village lately and more
distress than usual, which makes us more sorry to go, having been so
much interrupted in our proceedings there. We have been going our
rounds today and came home in the dark, paddling the muddy fields
with dim visions of cows rushing about. Whilst we were in the village
we stepped in to ask the old clergyman something and found him
with his dessert on the table and an elegant black man with an
embroidered shirt and woolly hair sitting by the fire. We were quite
startled and thought it was an apparition and sort of nightmare.
But he got up and made low graceful bows to us all and we discovered
he was the slave from Lord Holland's Jamaican estates who is come
over to learn the English way of working that he may persuade the
other slaves that all people here are not idle.

We are going to be quite full of company to overflowing for a few
days and then we shall be quiet for a week and then, woe is me, we
must e'en return to smoky Park Street and leave behind all romantic
ideas—funguses—rides—O it is heartrending to think of it.

Goodbye, dearest Aunt Fanny. Weep for me and believe me

Your very affectionate niece

C.P.

Cecilia ends her journal on her twenty-first birthday, 1840: "I am
very old and feel so. I had lovely presents such as the Queen might
envy and everything done to give me pleasure—in short there is no
end to the blessings bestowed on me. Mr. S. S.'s lines wounded me

but I tried to heal it with good thoughts." This refers to a poem written, I suppose, by Sydney Smith. It is very long and not very good, and I can understand how it hurt Cecilia. I quote only the first and last verses:

> Tell me which is the fairer maid,
> Dawn or midnight—sparkle or shade,
> Vivid rapture or placid bliss,
> Sunny Mary or Moonlight Ciss?
>
> Let those whose life is warm and bright
> Worship the pale and pure moonlight,
> But mine is icy chill—and I
> Must have some sunshine or I die.

CHAPTER FOUR

The Ridleys

CECILIA married Sir Matthew White Ridley, fourth Baronet, on 21 September 1841. Born in 1807, he was twelve years older than she was and a very rich and eligible young man.

He was the third child and eldest son of Sir Matthew White Ridley, third Baronet, of Blagdon in the county of Northumberland. The Ridleys were a very old and influential family in the North. The earliest reference to the family records that they owned extensive lands in the Tyne valley in 1154. They lived in what is locally known as a Pele Tower, or fortified manor house, called Willimoteswick, overlooking the South Tyne near Bardon Mill, and they took an active part in the border wars and family feuds that beset Northumberland throughout the Middle Ages. It was here that Nicholas Ridley, the Martyr Bishop of London, was born about 1503, and it was to his "Sister at Unthank" Hall, nearby, that he wrote the night before he was burnt at Oxford by Bloody Mary in 1555.

Willimoteswick was held by the Ridleys through a succession of "Broad Knights" until 1652, when Musgrave Ridley, in consequence of his loyalty to Charles the First, had all his lands confiscated by the Parliament. Musgrave died without issue, but the line continued through his first cousin Nicholas, who went to live in the nearby town of Newcastle-upon-Tyne. There the same spirit of adventure and acquisitiveness that was bred in him through the years of border war was applied to the developing coal trade. It must have been exciting to be alive in the North of England at that time. The rapid industrial developments which followed the early organisation of the coal trade gave enormous opportunities to young men of energy, enterprise and adventure.

Nicholas was only nineteen when he came to Newcastle, but he soon became an eminent coal-merchant and owner of coal-mines, for he was admitted to the powerful Company of Hostmen the following year. This famous Company had acquired the entire monopoly for the "Governance, and Control of the Loading, Unloading, and better Disposing, Selling and Vending of Sea Coals, and Pit Coals, Grindstones, Whetstones, and other Stones, within the River and Harbour of Tyne." The Hostmen, in short, controlled the whole of the trade and industry of Tyneside.

Membership of the Company carried also civic responsibility, of which Nicholas took his full share. He was Mayor of the City twice: first in 1688, the year of the "Glorious Revolution" and the landing of William of Orange, and again in 1707, another auspicious year when the Treaty of Union between England and Scotland was signed and peace came at last to the troubled border.

Nicholas died in 1710 and was succeeded in the business he had built up by his second son Richard. He was a man of great independence who has been described by Professor Hughes[1] as the "stormy petrel of the coal trade," for his refusal to join in any alliance to regulate the terms and conditions of the trade. He was extremely ambitious and perhaps not always scrupulous, but the weekly costs at his collieries were £600, and his rapidly expanding business was precariously dependent on the vagaries of weather to get the coal-ships out of the Tyne, to say nothing of the activities of the Pretender, so it is understandable that he could not always meet his creditors or pay the interest on the capital he borrowed.

In spite of his avowed reluctance to "stretch my arm beyond my coat sleeve," he was generous and kind and a good employer, and he made a lot of money eventually owing to his foresight and imagination in installing steam-engines in his pits to pump out the water and thus enable the coal to be mined at a much greater depth than had been possible before. These were the first steam-engines to be used in the North of England and he acquired the patent as early as 1729, which reveals the measure of his progressive and adventurous nature.

[1] *North Country Life in the Eighteenth Century*, by Edward Hughes (1952).

With his newly acquired wealth Richard bought a large estate at Heaton, now a suburb of Newcastle but at that time well beyond the city walls. Here he built a large and, for the period, curiously ugly mansion which was pulled down in 1936 to make way for a Council housing estate.

He married Margaret, a daughter of Matthew White, a fellow-merchant and coal-owner and a citizen of repute. Matthew White had come to Newcastle from Hawthorn, in County Durham, about the same time as Nicholas Ridley, and the two families were closely associated with each other from that time. In 1700 White bought the property of Blagdon, ten miles north of Newcastle, probably as a speculation for the coal underneath it rather than as a residence. There is nothing left of the original small manor house, which was pulled down either by his son or grandson, both of whom were called Matthew. But it is more likely that the grandson built the present house about 1750, for his mother's arms are quartered with White's in a beautifully carved coat in a stone scroll in the pediment on the south front. The architect of the house is unknown. He was probably a local man and it was a fine example of eighteenth-century architecture before it suffered, as the years went by, from the additions and alterations of succeeding generations, until in 1944 a fire gave opportunity to some extent to restore it to its original size and shape.

Richard Ridley died in 1739 and was succeeded by his son Matthew, who followed closely in the footsteps of his father and grandfather. He was an exceptionally intelligent boy, and, like his ancestor the Bishop, was sent south for his education. He went to Westminster and St. John's College, Oxford, where he matriculated in 1727 at the age of sixteen. He was called to the Bar in 1732 but does not seem to have practised at any time, and indeed he entered so young into the public life of Newcastle that he could not have had time to do so. He became Mayor in 1733, at the age of twenty-two, being probably the youngest man who ever occupied that exalted position.

In 1741 he entered Parliament as a Whig and he represented Newcastle through four successive parliaments until 1768 when he resigned in favour of his son. He was Mayor of Newcastle again in

1745, when the responsibility fell upon him to organise the defences of the town against the threatened invasion by the Young Pretender. For this "Loyalty and good Conduct" he was assured by H.R.H. the Duke of Cumberland that he had earned "the particular thanks" of his "Royal Father," George the Second. He did not, however, receive any more tangible honour or reward for this service, while his first cousin, the third Matthew White, was created a Baronet, probably by purchase, though he commanded the Militia at Berwick during the Rebellion.

Matthew Ridley married twice. His first wife was Hannah Barnes, and although she inherited a fortune of £800 from her father who was a respectable lawyer and citizen of Newcastle, the marriage took place clandestinely in London and was never made public during her lifetime, for a reason I have been unable to discover. From letters from them both which survive, it is evident that she was just as anxious as he was to keep the secret of their marriage, since disclosure would expose him to the risk of being "murdered in the dark." But by whom and for what reason remains a mystery. When she died in 1741, leaving a little boy of six her brother angrily accused Matthew of hastening her death by his harsh treatment of her. Even the little boy, Richard, is said to have taken up the cudgels on his mother's behalf, and brandishing a wooden sword in his father's face, cried "Now let me see who dare call my mother a whore."

A year after the death of poor Hannah, Matthew married his first cousin, Elizabeth White of Blagdon. This marriage was more fruitful, and, one hopes, happier than the first. It united the families of White and Ridley for the second generation, and on the death of her unmarried brother, Sir Matthew White, in 1763, the estate of Blagdon passed to Elizabeth with remainder to her eldest son, who also inherited the baronetcy and became Sir Matthew White Ridley. He also inherited Heaton, his elder half-brother Richard having given up all right and title to the estate, most likely for an annuity. Richard remained, however, very fond of all his half-brothers and half-sisters and was a constant visitor to Blagdon, even bequeathing to his half-brother the kidney-stone from which he died!

Sir Matthew White Ridley, second Baronet, was the third of the twelve children born to Matthew and Elizabeth, and appears from his portraits by Zoffany and Hoppner to have been a most attractive man. He was also a very gay one and was tried for adultery on one occasion and found guilty of "criminal conversation" with the wife of a Dr. Bromel on the staircase of her house in Newcastle and had to pay £400 damages. This little incident did not, however, affect his public career in the least. He was Mayor of Newcastle and Member of Parliament at the time, and he continued to enjoy the confidence and affection of the people in the North, and the reputation of a man of honour and respectability.

He married, in 1777, Sarah, daughter of Benjamin Colborne, a wealthy apothecary and landowner in Bath. They had seven children —six sons, and one daughter, who married John Scott, son of the Lord Chancellor Eldon. The second son, Nicholas, who was a Master in Chancery, inherited all the Bath property from his maternal grandfather and took the name of Colborne, eventually being created Baron Colborne for his political services. The third son died young and the remaining three all became clergymen.

The second Baronet died in 1813 and was succeeded by his eldest son, christened inevitably Matthew White. With a monotonous similarity he followed the family pattern, going to Westminster School and taking his B.A. at Oxford in 1798. In 1800 he did the Grand Tour of Europe, remaining abroad for fourteen months and then settling down at Heaton to manage the family business of collieries, glass-works, bank and the port of Blyth, while he also took part in local government, yeomanry and estate management. He was, however, far more of a countryman than any of his predecessors, and it was he who founded the pack of foxhounds that were later immortalised by Surtees, both in *Handley Cross* and *Hillingdon Hall* (where he says "Sir Mattha's hounds threw off at Gosforth Gates").

He married in 1803 Laura, only daughter of Dr. Hawkins, who was King's Surgeon to George the Third. He died soon after Laura's birth, and her mother married again a Mr. Bowater, by whom she had one son, Edward, who was eventually knighted for his service in the House of Commons.

Laura was the most extraordinary character. I think she was probably a little mad and she was certainly very unpleasant. During her early married life her constant child-bearing seems to have kept her eccentricities in abeyance, though it may have soured her temper, for she was not at all maternal. In her commonplace book she quoted the following words: "A family is seldom a community established for mutual advantage. Rivalry amongst the girls, competition amongst the boys, destroys harmony and provokes jealousy; and then, like the Ancients, we are left in the end, quite, quite alone in the wide, wide world."

"MOST TRUE" was Laura's comment, a contrast to the attitude of these days of dwindling families, when The Family is regarded almost with reverence as an institution for the rearing of children.

In the course of sixteen years Laura bore twelve children, ten of whom survived, which was remarkable for those days, and may partly be attributed to the fact that her mother-in-law was one of the earliest advocates of vaccination. It is recorded in the local newspaper as early as 1791 that "Lady Ridley has given directions that all the poor children in the Parish of Stannington, whose parents were willing, should be inoculated at her expense, and that upwards of sixty had received the benefit of her Ladyship's benevolence and were recovered." This was seven years before Jenner published his first treatise, and inoculation against smallpox was by no means the harmless procedure of today. Previous generations had suffered such appalling calamities from the disease that, however drastic the prevention, it must have seemed like a miracle when the first of the infectious fevers succumbed to the researches of science.

In 1813 when the second Baronet died, his son, Matthew White, the third Baronet, and his wife moved to Blagdon from Heaton, where they had spent the first ten years of their married life. They immediately set about enlarging the house to fit their family. With no respect for the symmetry and grace of its original architecture, they added a large dining-room on one side and a long, ungainly nursery wing on the other. They also found the London house in Portland Place, which the family had bought in 1792, too small or too unpretentious for their needs—for I think that Laura suffered

CECILIA'S MOTHER-IN-LAW

from *folie de grandeur* among other faults—and in 1827 they bought a site in Carlton House Terrace and built a house there for £15,000. Nash, who designed the Terrace, prepared plans for the inside also (which are still at Blagdon) but they were almost entirely altered by Ignatius Bonomi, an architect from Durham.

Considering the time in which they lived, a period of architecture and interior decoration which is so much admired today, the third Baronet did not have very good taste. But the Regency tide was on the turn, and I feel sure that Laura would have been in the van of every fashion. That she had very decided views on houses and how they should be lived in, can be judged from a letter she wrote to her son in 1836, after her husband had died and she was living in London. He was at that time proposing to build two vast galleries at Blagdon to house replicas of the Elgin marbles—a proposal which was mercifully never carried out. In commenting on the plan Laura observes:

I doubt if I would have windows—even to the West. I should say not—better not—as to light damp and all harms to the various objects, and smoke also, as by opening them the fire dust is thrown all over and room dust also. Neither servants or friends ever consider this sort of thing—a feeling you can't give either— the light from above you would like I know. Many talk of view out but the most beautiful is seldom looked at and the greater part of the time in a room is after it is shut up. If at home of a morning it is generally for business or reading when there is no time or wish to look at a country—ever so good. But people run away very much with this idea and call it dull without.

She seems to have suffered from a marked photophobia, for she goes on to say:

As to lights—that is really one of the great difficulties in all houses and greatest expense. But I think it is not necessary to use all rooms at night. All being used in the daytime keeps all aired and comfortable, and fortunately having coals on the spot makes all the difference, for good fires you must always have, and in all the rooms, or you get cold smoke and it looks wretched and the said fires light for passing through to a certain extent.

It is strange to think that coals cost less than candles and were easier to come by.

Laura certainly practised what she preached, for she not only blocked up five windows on the south front but glazed many of the others with stained glass, which must have made the house intolerably dark; and on the occasion of one of her daughters being ordered by the doctor to winter abroad, Laura said "Rubbish," put double windows into her bedroom to "bottle up the summer air" and there incarcerated the poor girl all the winter.

She was an exceedingly restless person and never seemed able to settle anywhere. In spite of having Blagdon, Heaton and Carlton House Terrace, she was constantly renting houses at Hammersmith or Hampton Court for the summer, and she was much given to wintering abroad. After her husband died in 1836 this restlessness became even more pronounced, and during the twenty-eight years of her widowhood she never stayed more than two years in any one place. We hear of her at Cheltenham, Worthing, Bedford, Yarmouth, Brighton and St. Leonards-on-Sea, while she had no less than four houses in London at various times. In spite of all this travelling, and although she lived until 1864, she never went in a railway train, and she was so ignorant of trains that when driving past the railway embankment at Brighton with her grandson one day, she asked him if the train travelled inside the embankment or on top of it.

One cannot help feeling sorry for her inability to settle anywhere or find the home she wanted, though I have no doubt that she was very difficult to please. But her real tragedy, and in this she was entirely to blame, was her relationship with her children. She was a hard and domineering mother. She was referred to by the cottage people at Blagdon as "The Proud Lady," and the story goes that she used to make all the children dress up in their riding clothes and parade in the hall every morning, but she would take only one of them out riding with her, and the others had disconsolately to go back to their rooms and change. It is also said that she never allowed any of the children to leave the nursery or schoolroom or come down to the drawing-room, and that relatives staying at Blagdon had to see the children by stealth or risk her displeasure.

Why she treated the children in this manner, which was going even further than the current maxim of being seen but not heard demanded, it is impossible to know; but the climax came in 1836, six months after her husband's death, when two of the girls, Marianne and Janetta, left their mother, unable any longer to put up with her tyranny and bullying, and went to live with an elder sister who had married a wealthy banker called Martin Smith five years before. All the brothers and sisters, with the exception of her eldest son, who was either too weak or too fond to oppose his mother, took their side and supported Marianne and Janetta in this action, although Cecilia, who heard only her husband's opinion, says she thinks they behaved very ill in the way they did it. Be that as it may, their mother never forgave them, nor any of the other children who supported them. She never saw or spoke to any of these nine children again. Even when years later Charles and William, two of the younger sons, went to the Crimean War and begged to see their mother to say goodbye, she refused to see them. This ban extended even to their children, and although she was consistently kind to Cecilia's children, she would have nothing to do with their cousins.

Sir Matthew, as I have said, took his mother's side in this quarrel. This involved him in very strained relationships with all his brothers and sisters, which Cecilia did her best to ease. There is no doubt that he was genuinely fond of his mother, and after Cecilia's death they became even closer to each other. When Laura died in 1864 he wrote in his diary: "Her decease has created for me a blank and void and the absence of a daily interest of such a special nature that no after years can supply."

I have felt it necessary to describe Laura at some length as she influenced her son a great deal, and he also inherited her touchiness and propensity for quarrelling.

I must also describe his brothers and sisters, since they figure in

C.R.—D

Cecilia's letters. Sarah, the eldest, married in 1837 John Cookson of Meldon Park near Morpeth in Northumberland. Then came Laura, who married in 1835 Charles Atticus Monck (who later changed his name to Middleton) and lived at Belsay Castle, about fifteen miles from Blagdon. Matthew White was the third, followed by Louisa, who married Martin Smith in 1831. Next came Marianne, who married a penniless clergyman called Andrew Corbett and lived in Lincolnshire. Charles was next; he was a Colonel in the Grenadier Guards and was said to have been a good soldier. He married Harriet Browne, daughter of Lord Oranmore. Janetta was next, and she was the one the people at Blagdon loved the most: "She was very kind to us," they used to say, many years after she died. She married in 1843 Isaac Cookson, a cousin of Sarah's husband. Henry, the seventh child and third son, was in Holy Orders and was curate at Stannington, the parish in which Blagdon is situated, when Cecilia first went to live there, and he springs to life very vividly in her early letters. He married Georgina Bradford in 1846, and became Vicar of Stanton in County Durham. Then came William, whom Cecilia loved the best, and in fact he was the only one who was on sufficiently good terms with Sir Matthew to come often to Blagdon. Sir Matthew even offered to give him a horse to take with him to the Crimea, which he refused as he said the horse was "much too good", but with expressions of extreme gratitude. He served in the Scots Fusilier Guards and became Governor of Malta. He never married.[1] George was the youngest and he was never asked to Blagdon during Cecilia's lifetime. Later, in 1852, he stood for the Southern Division of Northumberland, "very improperly in the Radical interest without consulting me," as Sir Matthew complained. He was defeated, but was returned for Newcastle in the election of 1856 and sat in the House of Commons for four years as a Whig, although he was reputed to have been "a thorough Tory" in every other way.

I have left Cecilia's husband to the last. He was educated at Westminster and Christ Church, afterwards doing the Grand Tour, where

[1] I wonder if he is the Colonel William Ridley to whom Miss Howard left £100 "as a souvenir" in her will? See *Miss Howard and the Emperor* by Simone André Maurois (1957), page 148.

he learnt to speak French so fluently and idiomatically that when, many years later, he revisited Paris as an old man, he talked to a French soldier in the Tuileries Gardens without "the warrior discovering his nationality." On his father's death in 1836 he refused the offer to stand for Newcastle in his stead, thus breaking the long tradition, lasting eighty-nine years in direct descent, of the Ridley representation of Newcastle in the House of Commons. It is possible that he was alarmed at the prospect of an election after a very unpleasant incident that took place at his father's last election in 1835. On that occasion a "brutal mob" attacked him, cut the traces of his carriage as he was driving down the Sandgate and tried to push it into the river. He managed to escape and to "gallop off and get into an inn" as fast as he could. But it is also likely that Sir Matthew's chances of getting in as a Tory were remote, and as he was an excessively shy and retiring man, he was not tough enough to face the kind of mud-slinging campaign he would have encountered. Besides, he was a countryman to his finger-tips and hated the life of cities, to which membership of the House would inevitably have condemned him. It was for this reason that he also gave up the long connection with the bank of Sir Matthew White Ridley and Co., which had been founded by his grandfather, the second Baronet, about 1755, and which was the first regularly constituted country bank in England. But in selling his shares Sir Matthew proved himself to be wiser than he knew, for the bank very shortly afterwards became insolvent.

He also leased all the collieries which had previously been worked by his forebears.

Sir Matthew, therefore, severed all connection with Newcastle and business and civic responsibility and devoted himself exclusively to his large estates at Blagdon and Blyth. This he did magnificently. He was an excellent landlord and a skilled and knowledgeable farmer. He enriched the property with some wonderful farm-buildings which are still models of what such buildings should be. He also bred prize cattle on a very large scale, and was all his life a keen sportsman. He bought a grouse moor in North Northumberland and hunted regularly three days a week every season, much to Cecilia's annoyance, although, funnily enough, he sold "those tiresome hounds" soon after she died.

His only other interest was in sculpture. I have already described his plan to build a sculpture gallery at Blagdon, and he was a most generous patron of the Newcastle sculptor John Lough, declaring him to be the greatest sculptor since Michael Angelo. If this estimation had been correct, his successors would have much cause to bless him, for he filled the house and garden with monumental examples of that gentleman's work. For the rest I must leave him to emerge in his own and Cecilia's letters.

CHAPTER FIVE

Marriage

THERE is unfortunately no mention in Cecilia's own words of her meeting Sir Matthew in the summer of 1841, nor do I know how long they knew each other before they became engaged. It cannot have been more than a month or two; his eligibility obviously endeared him to Lady Parke and she was willing to dispense with long acquaintance and courtship. On 16 July she wrote to the Baron who was on circuit at Lincoln:

London

My dearest Hub, . . . Sir Matthew spoke to Cecilia on leaving the ball at Lady Dungannon's and requested to call upon me the next morning, and I accordingly appointed 12 o'clock and he came a little before. We had a long talk of an hour and then sent for his mother and altogether we did not separate until past 3 and he then decided that the right thing to do was to go to you at Lincoln and ask your consent. I ventured to say that I thought he need not go for it and that writing would answer all the purpose, but as he seemed to think the boon he had to ask was too great to be done in any other way than by a personal request I consented and he is to go to you as soon as he can despatch his business in London. He is to return with the answer to Ampthill when we shall be glad to see him quietly before he goes to Newcastle. I think he will not want any other society than ours and I shall be delighted to have him, and you will find that your prophecy of my never seeing anyone worthy of our darling child is erroneous, for I really believe he will make her perfectly happy. The more I have seen of him the more I approve and I am so very happy at seeing the pleased and satisfied look of our darling, who I feel assured will give her whole heart with her hand.

Lady Ridley was all kindness and she seems to have a strong prejudice in favour of Cecilia and to wish so well to her son that whoever he selected she gladly receives. I think we have been most truly favoured by Providence in this affair, for it seems in all ways so likely to make the happiness greater of our beloved Child than even her past undeviating happy life. I expect that Sir Matthew will be as good a Husband as you have been, and in saying this I have said all that the fondest Mother could desire for the dearest and best of children. The only drawback is the difference in the family, which, though no immediate prospect offers of being settled, still has a possibility of being so whenever a happy moment arrives. He has suffered much in the cause and I think his feelings must be respected, for by quietly talking the affair over you will see that great difficulties arise and perhaps a speedy arrangement could not easily be made. I think it will be best to speak with Lady Ridley by and by on the subject, and I hope she will come and stay with us, for I am sure she must have good in her to have gained so much affection from her son and I think he was quite right to support her. . . . I shall not annouce this affair until I see Sir Matthew again. Pray tell him that he may come to Ampthill, for I should like him to do so whilst the weather is fine and he may possibly squeeze out a day or two before he proceeds to Newcastle. I should like him to see Cecilia in the quiet of home, although he says truly of her that her mind is always quiet and possessed, as much so in a crowd as it could, in the quiet of the country. I cannot allow myself to think of the breaking up this affair will be of our happy family circle, but we must hope to see the darling as often as possible and I already feel so favourably disposed to Sir Matthew that I trust he may never feel disinclined to come to us.

I must not take up your time, dearest Husband, for you will have to talk at length with Sir Matthew. I hope this may reach you first. I remain here until Tuesday morning and hope to be at Ampthill by 1 o'clock. We have written to prepare the room for Sir M. I have the key of the cellar.

[Sir Matthew went to Ampthill on 9 August 1841. The next day Lady Parke wrote again to her husband:]

Ampthill Park

Sir Matthew arrived about 5 and he has climaticised here as nicely as possible and my only regret will be parting with him, which we must do on Friday morning. He intends going to see my mother at York, which is his own proposal. He seems so very amiable and considerate to do all that is likely to give pleasure I really feel that he will make our darling happy and we must be thankful that such a happy lot is hers instead of a doubtful one which I think would have been the case with Granville Vernon, etc., etc., etc., etc., etc. However, with a thorough sense of this I still cannot help having sorrowful thoughts at the prospect of losing such a darling. I shall do my utmost to make Sir M. fond of us that we may induce him to be as much with us as possible.

He was charmed by your reception of him and your kindness and he looks the picture of happiness. I hope he will return to us again as soon as the Assizes are over. He is busy writing to all the members of his family with whom he is upon terms.

. . . I think Sir Matthew a very cultivated person and quite clever enough. I agree with Emily Hibbert who said O I hate your very superior men for husbands, they have so many drawbacks, and I think in this case that Sir M. is such a happy combination of good sense and useful qualities with as much information as a country gentleman can require and much more cultivation than they usually possess. I had much talk with him yesterday on the subject of a reconciliation and he has written to his mother on the subject and I trust the result may be satisfactory, although I shall not be surprised if it should not be so.

[It was not so. Neither Lady Parke nor Cecilia was ever able to effect a reconciliation between Lady Ridley and her children, and Lady Ridley was the only member of the family to be present at the wedding, which took place at Ampthill on 21 September.

Next day Mary Parke wrote to Aunt Fanny to say "the wedding went off as well as possible and all things were just as they ought to be. The day was perfect—'nor overdark nor overbright'—and just as one might wish. The Duchess of Bedford came not to my great joy. . . . Dear Cecilia was very composed and looked lovely. She came back here afterwards, as it was decided to be better for her to change her attire before travelling. Archdeacon Bailey gave us rather too long a service, as he read it all through, but he did it very well.

After they were gone we strolled up to Houghton and there Charlotte Denison,[1] Mr. Dundas and I sat all the afternoon conversing upon many subjects. I never knew him so charming, sensible and reasonable as he was and never liked him so well altogether as upon this visit. The evening was lovely and the repose of the whole thing delightful. All the school children came to tea and played on the lawn afterwards, and in the evening the servants had a dance and were much entertained and we passed our time in hunting out bits of Shakespeare and enjoyed our evening like our Sundays of old, than which nothing is pleasanter.''

Next day Cecilia wrote to her mother from Burford Bridge, where they spent the first night on their way to their honeymoon at Shoreham:]

I had no time to write last night. We arrived here at half past seven having had a delightful journey, everything as comfortable as possible and myself as happy as you could wish me to be. They gave us two post-boys with red and yellow racing jackets at St. Alban's, but with these we went but slowly, the goodness of the turn-out being all centred in the said jackets. We passed our door in Park Street, and I looked out thinking I might perchance discover the fair face of Miss Maria behind one of the dusty windows; however, she was I supposed better occupied. We changed in a *twink* by Vauxhall Bridge and got here it seemed to me very quickly. Heseltine[2] began forthwith to Mylady me and assumed an unbounded respect for me. She poured out "your Ladyship" at every instant and bowed most deferentially, which very much amused me; it required all my self-control to keep my countenance, which however I did and I feel ex-

---

[1] Charlotte Denison was a great friend and contemporary of Cecilia's. She was the youngest of the fourteen children of John Denison of Ossington, Notts. She married Robert Joseph Phillimore.

[2] Her maid who figures largely in her letters from now on.

CECILIA

HER HUSBAND

ceedingly majestic. All my silver concerns I had put out in grand style and on the whole I have been a very respectable "Ladyship."

This is a nice little spot just under Boxhill with a little quiet garden into which our sitting room opens. Sir Matthew sends you his best love and desires Papa will let him know soon whether he has heard about the dogs. He—that is Sir Matthew—is quite a pet and you have no idea how happy I feel, dearest Mama, although it was a bitter pang to me to leave my dear home.

Farewell dearest beloved mother.

Your very affectionate happy child
Cecilia Ridley.

[The following letters were written to Lady Parke from Rock House, Washington, near Shoreham.]

Thursday morning. 23 September 1841   *Shoreham*

You have no idea of anything half so charming as this dear little place. I verily believe it was made on purpose for us, it is so exactly what we like in every way. We arrived here for luncheon yesterday and had a most energetic greeting from Mrs. Malloch,[1] who poured out a great deal of Scotch talk and seemed very anxious and fussy. She had been to Worthing in a light cart to bring a few *essentials*, she said, which I believe consisted in foot tubs and sponge cakes, but alas she has altogether omitted *tin* tubs which we both think very essential to our happiness, so two have been summoned from Carlton Terrace and will soon arrive I hope. She has made the house look quite snug and comfortable but still she keeps apologising for the want of smartness. She was very anxious to know what *My Lady* liked for breakfast and got me some prawns. She is in a great rage with the oilman in town for not having sent some scraped beef which was ordered and she declares she *will* make him pay the carriage of it to punish him. The house is small but very clean—the outside very white, with a very blue slated roof, a door in the middle (N.B. no knocker on it) and two windows on each side. Then there is a little snug garden at the back and the whole is on the edge of a fine wild

[1] The housekeeper from Carlton House Terrace.

common which is quite enchanting. We went out and had a stroll on it yesterday and I never enjoyed anything so much. I long to find myself on the top of the downs but today is so boisterous that I think we must keep in the lower regions. From the window of our little drawing room where I am sitting now there is a pretty little peep of Washington church at the foot of a hill, and beyond that we see only our garden in which there is no great choice of flowers, but such as there are, Heseltine has gathered and put into a small glass on my dressing table, which I considered a very delicate attention on her part. The said damsel is very orderly and comfortable. I have given her some work to do and strict orders about sitting in her room. I make her keep my dressing table in great order and I have brought down several of my *writing table* presents to adorn our room, which really looks as snug and nice as possible. Lady Ridley has sent down her own teapot and coffeepot and silver candlesticks by the House-keeper, which I think very nice and kind of her.

We have read a little of Schiller and a little of Milton and I am rather pining for my small wee Coleridge which I have left behind by mistake: however I can do without it till we go back to Ampthill. I must tell you that those of my gowns which have been seen have been *excessively* approved—viz my Indian muslin and two lilac silks. I have made myself very smart with rings and chains and feel an extraordinary pleasure in decking myself out. What do you think of that?

If you have not cut the Blagdon pine[apple] yet pray do so forth-with, for we had ours yesterday and it was delicious. I think there was never anyone so fortunate, so blessed as I am. I do not mean because of the pine.

Your very affectionate grateful child

Cecilia Ridley.

[Sir Matthew also wrote to Lady Parke on the same day:]

Shoreham

My dear Lady Parke, Cecilia is writing to you and I add this note to assure you of her being most perfectly well and smiling happily and joyously as I write. She is pleased to approve our selected *séjour* and I have every hope of it suiting her in all respects. We have endeavoured to make her as comfortable as circumstances allowed and I am delighted in finding we have been so far successful. I am sure you would like the place for the occasion in question. My happiness and indeed ours is more than can be told, so I will not touch upon that theme and feel most strongly the moral conviction in my own mind that this our actual happiness will be, as regards ourselves, but the commencement of a series of happy years if we both, please God, be spared. That this our happiness will add to yours, the Baron's and to Cecilia's own we all must feel, and with every affectionate remembrance to the Baron, Mary and Alice and every wish for your having at last recovered your composure after the trial and excitement of recent events. Believe me affectionately yours

Matt White Ridley.

25 September 1841 *Shoreham*

Dearest Mama, I did not write yesterday, feeling idle and having nothing particular to say and some other epistles to concoct. Mrs. Morier[1] had written to me from Brighton begging that we would go over and lunch with her, but we both felt so much averse to it that I was e'en obliged to sit down and compose as amiable an apology as best I could—and indeed I felt that Mrs. M. ought not to expect us to show ourselves in so public a way so very soon. I hope she will not be offended and withhold her gracious favour from us. Thank you very much for your dear nice letter, it is a great delight to me to hear from you. But yet I must beg that you will go out and walk another time instead of writing so much, for I would willingly give up the pleasure of a letter to give you a little air and exercise. So in return for your advice to me on the subject of health I must entreat that *you* will go out every day, as it is very bad for you to stay scribbling at home. Sir M. is made quite uneasy by the thought of your want of

[1] Mrs. Morier was the wife of James Justinian Morier, diplomat, traveller, author of *Hajji Baba of Ispahan*, considered by Sir Walter Scott to be the finest novelist of his day. She was a daughter of William Fulke Greville and first cousin to the diarist.

air, so be a good mother and take care of yourself. I assure you I am a model of prudence about myself, and my *husband* takes every possible care of me.

Yesterday we went to Worthing to do some shopping and take a quiet stroll on the seashore. I am overjoyed that we are here instead of there, for there are quantities of folks there and it is all public and staring. Whilst we were waiting at a shop door Lord and Lady Marcus Hill[1] passed by and presently there came Captain Blake, her ladyship's brother, with his facetious rubicund countenance and actually ventured to bow to me, which made me feel very shy and queer. I returned his bow however but somewhat stiffly, being seized with a great fear that he would come and speak to me, which however he forbore to do. Sir M. met with a friend, Col. Broadhead, and Mr. Elwes was to be seen parading the streets and eyeing us with curiosity—like the little wren—but we had no conversation with anyone. We bought pigeons, a rabbit, candles and all manner of oddments and were rather puzzled as to whether the rabbit should be skinned and prepared by the man or be done at home. Sir M. looked very grave and judgelike when the question was propounded and with due pomp decided at length to his own satisfaction and I have no doubt to that of the rabbit and the poulterer also. We walked on a retired part of the beach up and down but it was a *muggy* evening and no breeze from the sea. We watched the little sand-coloured crabs and teased all that came in our way and we canvassed two fishermen digging for baits with unlooked-for success. I saw no shells nor pebbles.

From Sir Matthew to the Baron
28 September 1841   *Shoreham*
My dear Sir, I am writing in the most wet windy and gusty day you can imagine, but Cecilia's countenance is such a beaming and beautiful and joyous landscape that I have little or no thought for

[1] Lord Marcus Hill married in 1837 Louisa, daughter of Joseph Blake, a descendant of the Admiral. In 1861 he obtained a Royal Licence to take the title of Baron Sandys, which he inherited from his mother, the Marchioness of Downshire.

what the elements are about, in so far at least as their good or evil humour bears upon our happiness at this present moment. That this happiness will be a lasting one I have a moral conviction, and it will be such, I fervently trust, as will add to your own and to all connected with the loved being so lately and so solemnly made mine. How proud I am in possessing her none can know or how much all her endearing and companionable qualities and excellencies win more and more hourly upon me. . . . As regards the dogs I hope they may be useful. The little dog will probably prove the best. You will find Ben, I think, very useful for pheasants in hedgerows.

We have had our ride each day till today. Yesterday evening we arrived at home rather later than usual after a long but *unsuccessful canvass*. I never saw such a set of uncivil brutes as many in this district, in refusing an answer to a question however civilly put. I have no chance I see for Sussex. I find they feasted and danced in two days about 320 at Blagdon, and they seem to have enjoyed themselves . . . My groom has unfortunately gone out of his mind which is a sad example, but has fortunately been recovered in his wanderings by his relatives. It was feared that he had destroyed himself. No reason can be assigned I believe—a sober creature, very, and apparently very comfortable and happy with his wife and family.

29 September 1841   *Shoreham*

Dear Lady Parke,

I intended writing you at an earlier hour than $\frac{1}{2}$ an hour before post, but a heavy northern post requiring attention has forestalled you and you may now not get much. In addition to the post Cecilia has been so arch, and so full of "quips and cranks and wanton wiles" for some time, that my attention has been somewhat distracted. I must thank you sincerely for your very kind note, and express how really gratified I am at your entertaining in common with the Baron a confident expectation of Cecilia's finding a permanently happy home with me. I truly and firmly believe that as years roll on we shall, if we be spared, become still more, if possible, attached to each other than we are, and two beings more happy in each other's society than we are no imagination could picture and no reality supply. My appreciation of your dear child daily increases, as does my conviction of my capability of ensuring her happiness, and I can write you in the fullest and most confident reliance on this most important and interesting topic. I have been much gratified, I can assure you, at your cheerful account, and you may believe me when I say that I can in fancy see the chasm I might make in your circle. Nevertheless this vacancy will I trust frequently be supplied for intervals of enjoyment, and your knowledge of her contentment and happy feelings as my much cherished wife and friend will in softening the regret arising from the blank of her absence eventually add to your own enjoyment and that of all those dear relatives whom she has lately left. Further, I sincerely trust that our own relation to each other may daily and yearly improve, and you may rely upon it that I can never look upon Cecilia's parents with other feelings than those I do now by those of gratitude and affection. Time will show whether I know, by our feelings. I fearlessly abide the trial. Excuse rapid writing. By the way Cecilia desires I will say *the tip of her nose is quite cool*. This I have impressed her is a sure sign of health. I am certain you would think her looking remarkably well. I am not quite sure about her being a Madonna—sometimes she is a Sunny Landscape in fair Italy, sometimes a Symphony in Music, sometimes an exquisitely harmonious picture—a glowing but tempered Claude, sometimes like one from another world, but at all times your dear and darling child and my sincerely and truly loved companion. Now adieu, believe how happy we both are in the present and how confident in the future and how affectionately yours,

                                        M. W. R. and C. A. R.

30 September 1841   *Shoreham*

Dearest Mama . . . There is an account in the Newcastle paper today of the ringing of all bells on the 21st, which brought visions of long bills from bellringers to our minds . . .

There has been a small affair of honour about towels. I found only very fine smooth ones in my room and requested that I might be permitted to have rough ones, which I discovered was a great mortification to Mrs. Malloch who had had these fine articles especially woven for me. I therefore mean to have some for my face and hands, which will be a desirable arrangement I think. Mrs. M. makes capital orange marmalade and excellent barley water which rivals Papa's yellow bottle. . . . Nothing could be more attentive than Heseltine—she takes great care of me and is tidiness and regularity itself. She has done a reasonable quantity of work and I really feel that I have got a treasure. Bateman too is all attention and activity. He does almost all the waiting himself and very well and looks quite blooming and beautiful with his exertions. No fair Sophia could resist him now I am sure, and if I were to see him in the hollow oak I should take him for a Mr. Dryad, so brilliant and fair is his appearance.

Would you like to have a specimen of our dinners? Enter first two whitings. They are devoured all but their heads and tails, which depart bereaved of their bodies. Enter next a roast partridge which is placed before me and a small wee bit of lamb before Sir Matthew. We both offer each other some of our respective dishes in the civillest manner and end by each eating our own. N.B. very hot roasted potatoes. Departed the first course. Then enters a smoking pudding which we both look at but, feeling that duty to ourselves and each other forbids our eating any more, we send it away. Enter the cheese —after which the fifth and last act of the play, a sumptuous dessert —grapes, pine, brandy cherries, cakes, French plums. Here, as in all dramas, is the chief interest of the day centred and here are many of the characters put an end to. The grapes I murder are without end but the stock seems to be like the magic purse, for fresh ones always appear, and I hope they will go on till we get some more for they are so good.

My little writing case is quite a pet. It gets very *thin* here with all this good air and hard *writing* and I must take measures to restore its former stoutness. I have made various discoveries, amongst which is that I see Sir Matthew's nose is crooked—a fact which I believe even Lady Ridley is not aware of. I forgot to mention, as one of the ornaments of our room, an elegant little extinguisher the handle of which is a beautiful frosted fox creeping up and looking wistfully at a cock perched at the top. It is a dear little funny thing and was a present of Lady Ridley to *Matt*, for I mean to call him so now IF I can summon courage. Your very affectionate child Cecilia Ridley.

Monday, 4 October 1841   *Shoreham*
Dearest Papa, . . . We had a charming drive on Saturday to see Petworth. It is an odd strange place tacked on to the town with an immense high windowless wall like the Castle at York, at the end of which you enter what is called the Porter's Lodge. Here we were consigned to the care of a humpy old dame who led us along a passage "long and lank and brown as is the ribbed sea sand" (for which expression I am indebted to my friend Mr. Coleridge). At the end of this corridor the old dame delivered us up to a humpy little man who took us through other passages very twisting and mysterious till at last we emerged into a very magnificent hall. The house is immense and there are some very fine high rooms, all full of pictures ancient and modern, good and bad, sacred and profane, landscape and figures, jumbled together without any arrangement whatever. The walls, with the exception of two or three rooms, are quite unfinished—nothing but plaster of various brown and white hues, and it altogether struck me as being very like some old German palace, so rambling and uncomfortable looking. There is a fine gallery at the end of the house lighted from above and full of pictures and statues, many of which are by Carew who was patronised by Lord Egremont. But none very good, and the state of disorder in which the pictures are spoils their effect very much. We saw nothing of the family except a second little hunchback man who was wandering about seemingly very busy looking for something to do, which he evidently could not find. In one room there are copies of the Hampton Court beauties hanging round, and Col. Wyndham has unmercifully rolled up their legs to make room for some battle pieces below, which seems to me to be an odd thing to do. The park is not very pretty but very extensive and *neat*.

I am sorry you miss my Milton, but he is not leading an unprofitable life here, for we read him very often with great satisfaction.

All our books have had their turn, and we have bought a small *Childe Harold* that I may be introduced to the beauties of Byron. I assure you we spend our time in a sensible reasonable manner and keep very early wholesome hours: indeed in that respect we are quite an exAMPLE to you at Ampthill. We had a visit from Mrs. Chatfield, our landlady, the other day and tried to make ourselves very agreeable to her. She is a rich old farmer dame, very fat and in deep mourning, poor thing. She sat on a chair in the middle of the room, very much puzzled about her hands and arms, which appeared to be very much in the way and were very large and conspicuous. She seemed quite pleased with us on the whole and she testifies her regard by bringing offerings of flowers or partridges whenever she comes.

October 1841   *Shoreham*

Sir M. and I are in a state of feud and discord about the clergyman, to whom I take great objection for many weighty reasons. First because he preaches the same sermon at his two churches the same day. Second because he reads carelessly and looks indifferent. Thirdly because he is always going out shooting, and fourthly—because I do not like his looks. I see plainly we shall never agree about him. Is it not shocking that we should differ so?

Today after an early lunch we sallied forth for a down ride. We went up to the nearest point and cantered on and on for many miles till we got to a place called Amberley. Some of the squires in the neighbourhood were shooting rabbits on the heights with a pack of beagles and I thought it seemed most tempting sport. It is astonishing how little the *inhabitants* of this country seem to go up on the downs. We have never seen a single gentleman there until today when, besides the *beaglers*, there was a horseman in white trousers whom we decided to be the Hon. Rob Curzon[1] of Parham Park, who took a short gallop and then went down, on which account we judged him a heartless man, unworthy of the scene. When we came home

[1] The Hon. Robert Curzon (1774–1863), M.P., son of the first Viscount Curzon, married in 1808 Harriet Anne, Baroness de la Zouche in her own right.

we found the Hon. Rob had called here, and being desirous to satisfy our curiosity we demanded a description of him from the footman and found that he was not the Down Hero.

Wednesday, 13 October 1841   *Shoreham*

Yesterday we went to return the Hon. Rob's call. His place is charming, the park full of wild fern and old trees and stags with huge horns sitting or standing in attitudes just as they ought. In short a sort of *As You Like It* scene. The house is old and grey— mullion windows, gable ends, antique chimneys, the entrance door arched and massive with a courtyard and a fountain playing in the centre—quite enchanting to behold. We stood in front of the massive door and rang and then waited in expectation of some picturesque figure of a porter descending the time-worn steps with dignity and grace. We waited long. At last there was a rumbling noise heard in the inside, of bolts and bars, which seemed not much inclined to move. However at last they gave way and behold a shabby old rickety teakettle issued forth in a dirty livery, no speculation in his eyes, no powder in his hair, no smartness in his figure, no grace in his bearing. Immediately bright vivid pictures of the whole establish- ment rose before our eyes. I see, at this very moment, the Honourable Mrs. Robert wrapped in whittles,[1] with a very pale face and a very plain cap, eating a sweetbread done white. I see her, as it is very fine, pulling a string attached to the bell and telling the old brown teakettle that she will take an airing in her poney chay. I see her, clad in more whittles than before, her head covered by an old white silk bonnet and a brown veil, slowly descend the old manorial stair- case. The teakettle tucks her into a carriage and she is dragged gently along one of the roads in the park, as far as the lodge and back. In the evening she is rather tired and the Hon. Rob reads the news- paper, takes a nap and says a word or two about the new people at Rock House. Mrs. R. all this time reclining on a sopha working a kettle-holder in a very simple pattern. Poor thing, I am sure she never goes on to the downs.

[1] A dialect word meaning shawls or wraps.

October 1841   *Shoreham*

Bismillah, how it rains! There is a sort of reservoir over the portico which is now brimful of water just under Sir Matthew's dressing room window and he experiences every morning a sore temptation to jump into it, only unfortunately he *might* be seen by the Worthing coach for about a minute from the road. He says he should only be taken for a statue, but on the whole we think it advisable and respectable not to do it, so I think he will resist. . . . There has been a most tender epistle from the Rev. Richard Ridley[1] and the answer is at present concocting on the other side of the table, offering to pay them a small visit on the 23rd of October. We think we shall be with you at Ampthill from the 16th to the 21st and stay the 22nd evening at York and so be at Blagdon on the 25th and have a few days quiet before the hunting and other bothers begin.

[The journey from London to Blagdon took three days and must have been a most trying and weary business, even when taken in easy stages and staying with relatives on the way. Cecilia and her husband spent a few days at Ampthill and the farewell must have been even more of a wrench than at the time of her marriage, for this time she was going away to live three hundred miles from her beloved family. She had never seen her future home, so that her dread must have been mingled with a certain excitement. She wrote to her mother from York:]

We arrived here in capital time and found all very flourishing. Grandma has a cold but she came down in the evening, looked well and was brimful of fun and quite delighted with your cape. She kept telling Sir M. he was lovely and did nothing but admire his countenance all evening. . . . Aunts Fanny and Marianne are civil to each other and look well—both quite pleased with their caps. Aunt Ma has got the one without strings and thinks it very fashionable and the crack thing.

[1] Sir Matthew's uncle. Fourth son of the second Baronet, he married in 1810 Catherine Lucy, daughter of John Popplewell Johnson. He was Rector of Leathley, Yorks.

CHAPTER SIX

Blagdon

BLAGDON today looks very much the same as when Cecilia arrived there for the first time. The colour of the stone, quarried from the ground two hundred yards from the house, may have darkened a little with a century's smoke from the nearby colliery of Seaton Burn, but the later additions built by Cecilia's son in 1890 were pulled down in 1947, while the long nursery wing built by her mother-in-law in 1820 still remains. The layout of the gardens has changed and many of the trees she saw as saplings have now reached full maturity. Inside the house the arrangement of the rooms is just the same, with the exception of the kitchen which has moved seven times since her day and has still not found its final destination; and eleven of the forty bedrooms have since been converted into bathrooms. Much of the furniture Cecilia would recognise, though a few pieces I had to rescue from the servants' quarters and stables, to which they had been consigned by later generations, and some of the books in the library are those she read: the second folio Shakespeare, for instance, that she mentions in her first letter.

The descendants of many of the neighbours named in the following letters are still in the county and living in the same houses. People still dance at Alnwick Castle and the Assembly Rooms in Newcastle, and the same cold winds drive the heavy clouds across the moors while the Tyne fret stretches from the sea. The advent of trains, cars and aeroplanes has not really made it feel any nearer to London, or so it seemed to me when I also left my family in the south and came to live at Blagdon eighty years later. I also arrived on a late October evening and wrote the next day to my mother in equal awe of the housekeeper who had been there for twenty years.

BLAGDON, 1954

Tuesday, 26 October 1841   *Blagdon*

Dearest Mama, Here I am settled in my future home—or rather not at all settled yet, but soon to be so, I hope. We got here yesterday, after a wet journey, and Sir Matthew's interview with his groom at Durham took so long a time that it was quite dark before we arrived even at Newcastle and therefore I could see nothing of the country. Mrs. Ridley gave us nothing but sponge biscuits and a roll in the carriage, which was very nasty of her I think. She and Mr. R. were very kind to me, but I confess, *entre nous*, I was rather disappointed with them. She is so queer and full of violent prejudices and so formal and he is so full of sporting that I did not feel to get on with him. With Mrs. I was more comfortable and I think she is a good woman but not pleasant. One thing that annoyed me a little was that she did nothing but abuse people I like; otherwise we agreed on some few subjects and I tried very hard to be agreeable to her.

Now for Blagdon. After breakfast this morning I sent for the house-keeper and went all over the house with her, saw every bedroom, servants' and all, housekeeper's room, stillroom, linen chests and looked through everything. The kitchens I shall go to another day, for I was tired and knocked up after my walk this morning. I was much pleased with everything and particularly with the housekeeper Mrs. Slight. I never saw a nicer looking woman with such good manners and apparently so much order and method. She and I agreed perfectly in our views of the spare bedrooms: never in my life have I seen such frightful hideosities of beds as they are—old dark stuffs chiefly in hideous shapes. I cannot stand it and certainly before another year I must do something. No, I never beheld such nasty old horrors, so do not expect a pretty bedroom when you come *this* time. They are capital rooms and a great many of them, and the house is very convenient and contains a greater number of chests of drawers and wardrobes than any place I ever saw. The best room is the dining room which is very handsome and has some beautiful pictures, as all the rooms have. The other three sitting rooms are all car-petted and curtained with red, plenty of nice tables and sofas about and very comfortable. Upstairs my three rooms are *delightful*, newly done up and very clean and nice. Sir M. has made a mistake in choosing the papers of the bedroom and dressing room; the carpets were new and had been put by, drab with blue flowers, and he has got a greeny paper for them, very nice in itself but not pretty with the blue carpet. The sitting room is charming, all fitted with oak, *delicious* tables and very nice carpet and the walls plain pale green with numbers of nice little pictures. I mean to keep nearly all my pretty things in that room, but the papier mâché I think I shall send into the drawing room. I have got an incredible quantity of drawers and closets in my rooms, all oak and very nice. I shall not near fill them. What quantities of *habiliments* my mother [in-law] must have had. I am so glad Lady R. thought of her own comfort so much; no other creature could have arranged such commodious concerns.

I am in the saloon at this moment writing. It has a high coved ceiling, very handsome, and three long French windows opening into a sort of outer room with a stone floor and windows partly of coloured glass. In this sort of portico there are plants and two statues. It does not go up to the height of the room, and above it there are three ground glass windows. I have made a lovely little sketch of the wall opposite me as I write and also a complete and highly finished plan of the house for your benefit. I should be very glad to have your prescriptions for medicines. I have not ordered dinner today and shall probably not tomorrow: perhaps the next day I may. Now and then I feel almost overwhelmed and wish I could make things stop for a day just to rest and to be as I was, but when I am quite settled I shall be very comfortable and soon get accustomed to it. I mean to make gradual alterations in the style of tea and coffee making, but I must not be in too great a hurry. Pearson is a tall man with drabbish hair and skin, holds himself gracefully and walks well; his manner is good and he seems to know his place. He was footman to Lord de Grey and I think I recollect his face. Priddle has an amazing presence: he is rather stout, good humoured looking and his manner most important. His walk across the room is astonishing. The under butler is immense *phat* and has a look of the fat boy; the other footman is very thin and nice looking. I am so glad you now speak in earnest about coming here. If you do not I really shall be in despair—I do not know what I shall do. Sir M. is gone out to see after work-men etc. and I am so tired I can do nothing but sit still and write which is very comfortable. I was presented to Mr. Turner, the agent, this morning, and when Sir M. said what a faithful attached man he was, he burst into tears, poor man, so it was altogether a very affecting interview.

The harp sounds charmingly in this room, so does the piano, and there is a lovely harp stand made by Gillow with fascinating brass feet that take up no room at all. Pray write me a letter soon full of advice about all sorts of things. It will be sure to be very acceptable. I hope I shall succeed in having prayers but do not feel sure. Goodbye, dearest Mama, love to all and tell dearest Mary we possess a second edition of Shakespeare here.

Thursday, 28 October *Blagdon*

I feel nearly settled now and extremely comfortable. I have now sent for the housekeeper and am going to talk over the tea making, so you see I am beginning well. Yesterday I went out—round the gardens and then to the kennels where I lionised all the hounds and saw them fed. The cleanliness and order of the place is not to be told. There are separate yards and separate bedrooms for the ladies and gentlemen and a dining room in the centre, into which they are called in one by one by their name, and none ventures to go before their name is called. Behind there are living houses for all the men and their wives, each with a little clean yard and store houses for the provisions required, and in course of time there will be little gardens laid out for each family. In short nothing can be nicer. The kitchen garden is very large; the flower garden not so, but quite large enough and in a pretty situation. I promise myself great pleasure in arranging it. The gardener looks comfortable and not fine and has a strong burr. The Duchess of Northumberland left her card yesterday on her way back to Alnwick from the bazaar at Newcastle. I have had no other visitors.[1]

[1] The third Duke of Northumberland married in 1817 Lady Charlotte Florentia Clive, daughter of the first Earl of Powis.

1 November 1841   *Blagdon*

I forget whether I told you of the sad event that occurred just after we arrived here. The groom, who had gone out of his mind before, came back to his place, apparently recovered, and was found one day drowned in a pond in the park. He was a very faithful and valuable servant to Matt and the inconvenience and trouble occasioned by his loss is endless, as there are thirty horses and no person equal to the charge of them. However that is nothing compared with the affliction of the poor widow who is left very ill provided for with three little children. Yesterday Matt had to go to Newcastle on business, so I was left alone all day. He told me not to go and see the poor widow, but I ascertained that it would be rather a satisfaction to her to see me, so I went, and a more melancholy scene I never witnessed. She is very composed, wonderfully so indeed. She was sitting in a corner of the room crying and rocking a cradle in which was a baby 4 months old, and two other lovely children were laughing and playing about her, quite unconscious of what had happened. They keep asking for their father and calling for him. They were very fond of him. The poor man had seemed quite well when he took possession of the stables, but the next day he said he found himself unequal to it and must give up. The day after that he seemed very nervous, they say. He walked out and would not let his children follow him as usual and was last seen talking to the blacksmith. Very soon after his wife followed him, being anxious about him, and went down to a piece of water in the park, where she saw his hat and then immediately gave the alarm. The pond was dragged and he was found—quite dead of course. The coroner's inquest was held yesterday and the verdict returned was "*insanity*." The widow's own father drowned himself a few years ago and her sister died in a madhouse. It is very sad but I shall say no more about it.

. . . I have had a few visitors but not seen many, as most came when I was out. Mrs. John Cookson came one day, and I went to see her afterwards. She seems a very amiable person and very domestic— not pretty but rather pleasing. I should not say she was agreeable exactly but there is nothing to dislike about her appearance or manner, and Henry Ridley lives in the village a mile and a half away and is a clergyman. I should say the good he has done since he has been here is not to be told, for the old Rector never went into any of the cottages, nor did his wife, and consequently they were neither liked nor respected. Henry does the duty as well as it can be done. He has a fine clear voice and a very good quiet manner and his sermons are very practical and impressive. The church is large and empty, which is not to be wondered at, as many of the people have to go miles. There *is* a stove but it is in a corner of the church next to our pew, which is the only one which receives the slightest benefit from it, so I mean to try and see if another could not be put there. I have not been to any of the houses in the village yet, but I have been to see the people about the place and shall make acquaintance with all these first. Stannington is a nasty, cheerless, untidy looking village, not attractive at all, although the people are none of them very poor and the cottages in general well built. Even the farmers appear to me to be very uncivilised; they have all excellent houses, but you never see a bit of garden about them, no look of comfort, no bee hives, no holly oaks as you see in Beds. I am sorry the village is so far. There is a good school, both every weekday and Sunday. Ninety boys and girls and a capital schoolmaster who acts as clerk and is seen first in the singing gallery giving out the psalms and lifting up his melodious voice amongst the schoolchildren and then hops down and takes his post under the Rev. Henry, all the time squinting horribly with a very sweet smile on his mouth.

21 November 1841   *Blagdon*

I have made a sort of plan of the flower garden and have the satisfaction of seeing that it is not a bit like it. I think the thing will be to have all the beds in the grass in patches or masses with a few rustic baskets, and to keep the tall flowers—lilies, dahlias and hollyhocks—to the border by the greenhouse, and other plans of that sort. The beds as they now are, are much too big for anything of that sort but you cannot judge by my silly plan. They were every one of them entirely full of dahlias last year . . .

There are some lovely walks here in a wood that skirts the park between the lodges. I really never saw anything prettier, and now the colouring on the beeches makes them look beautiful. I have been riding nearly every day and I have also walked about a great deal in spite of mud. I have some boots that defy all wet and I now feel very bold and independent and trudge about by myself with great comfort. I make my petticoats very dirty but never mind.

I am so glad you talk seriously of coming at Xmas. You cannot think how happy it makes me to think of having you here. I am afraid you must submit to sleep in a *stuff* bed.

November 1841   *Blagdon*

You had better not say a word to Lady Ridley about schools etc. I think. I see quite well the sort of person she has been from what I gather in the cottages about the place. I have not yet heard a word in her praise from anyone, rich or poor—they all preserve a strict silence on the subject. But whenever the first Lady's name[1] is mentioned there is universal love and praise. An old lady in whose house Henry lodges let out rather more about her than other people. I went to see her yesterday and she talked over all the Ridleys for generations past and present, and said concerning the late Lady, as she called her, that she had been a perfect beauty and certainly had always been kind to her but exacted a great deal of respect. The first Lady, she said, was not a beauty but then she was good.

By the bye, I want to know whether you like penwipers with white linen inside? They are all so here and the housekeeper renews them now and then. I think them very nasty, but Matt admires them, so that I think they will cause a divorce some day. Mrs. Slight made a biscuit this morning but it was all wrong and I fear I shall not make her understand, so you must bring one down when you come.

November 1841   *Blagdon*

Our party all arrived yesterday and I think we had a very sociable agreeable evening, thanks to my tea table, which I thought of wonderful use and advantage. Mrs. Cookson is very nice and looks quite like a lady and Matt is very kind to her. Mrs. Bell[2] is a wee bit

[1] Sir Matthew's grandmother, the first Lady Ridley.

[2] Mrs. Bell was the second wife of Robert Bell of Fenham Hall, now a school in the outskirts of Newcastle. She was Emma Donna, daughter

vulgar looking and Mrs. Adamson rather heavy. Mr. Adamson is
the best of the gentlemen, in my opinion.[1] There are two Mr. Cooksons and a Mr. James, all exactly like each other in three degrees of
height, with very high sloping foreheads and good humoured countenances. None of them very entertaining.

We played last night. Mrs. Cookson accompanied me on the
piano, at sight, quite beautifully, and really it was not dull. That
good old Mr. Adamson was so civil and kind and agreeable he quite
won my heart. He is going to lend me books and help me in all
sorts of ways. I have got Mr. Richardson's address[2] and I find he will
not object to coming here to teach, but I think I cannot have him and
I will tell you why. I have been asking Matt about my money and
he makes it out that I have only the pin money that comes from
my own fortune. I said I thought I had other money besides and he
said "Not that I know of. Your pin money is £300 a year according
to the settlement." I said no more, but if that is so I am going much
too fast and must stop. It is very odd and I do not understand it. Do
ask Papa, for I am sure, as it was explained to me, I expected that
Matt was to pay me another £350 a year separate. I feel very well
but rather stupid. I have been paying bills and talking so long that I
really must go and see after my guests lest they should think me a
bear. So goodbye, dearest Mama, for today.

November 1841   *Blagdon*

I enjoyed myself at Meldon and was very glad to be there and
make friends with my sister Cookson. She is a sensible, amiable
woman and wonderful considering her education and example, for she
fusses about and manages capitally and is a real good economical,

---

of Isaac Cookson of Whitehill. Robert Bell was the grandson of Matthew
Bell of Woolsington, Northumberland, and Jane Ridley, so that he was
a distant cousin to Sir Matthew.

[1] John Adamson (1787–1855), scholar and antiquary; founder of the
Newcastle Law Society, the Natural History Society and co-secretary of
the Literary and Philosophical Society. He married his cousin, Elizabeth
Huthwaite.

[2] Thomas Miles Richardson (1784–1847), a well-known Newcastle
painter in water-colour.

methodical wife. Not a person of much cultivation but she has qualities more valuable and is always happy and always busy. I thought it best to talk with her a little on the forbidden subject and I thought her very nice about her mother and about Matt, though evidently she is not a *very* affectionate sister, at least not towards all her brethren. Her children are very nice and well brought up. The eldest girl took a great fancy to me and said she should call her first child Cecilia. They say Janetta is to marry Mr. Isaac Cookson, Mr. John's cousin, which I shall be sorry for, as it will be an additional discord in the county. I never thought it would distress me so much as it does. Even Henry, although I like him and he is very useful to me and an excellent clergyman, I cannot help wishing far away sometimes, for there is no cordiality between him and Matt. Matt always calls him "that youth" and says he cannot bear having him here. Henry certainly had, and has I believe, not a good temper, but he seems to be much improved in that respect and does his duty very well. We are great friends and he has taken me through half the village and we shall do the other half the first frosty day. It is too wet.

6 December 1841 *Blagdon*

Dearest Aunt Fanny, I have often intended to write to you lately and always been prevented, which seems very odd, for I really can hardly understand myself how it is that I am so busy. I am now counting the hours till the day which is to bring my dear family here, which is rapidly approaching, and now I really begin to believe that they will come, which I was afraid of doing before. We are going to Alnwick for a few days this week, but hitherto we have been perfectly quiet with the exception of the numerous visits I have had to return. Amongst other places I went one day to Cresswell, where dwelleth the older brother of our Mr. Cresswell who is M.P. for the County and having married a very wealthy lady bought an estate here, and has created the place where he lives, entirely.[1] It is close to the sea

[1] John Addison Baker-Cresswell, of Cresswell, Northumberland (1788–1869). M.P. for Northumberland 1841–47; married 1818 Elizabeth Mary, daughter of Gilfrid Lawson Reed. Mr. Cresswell had four

which is very fine there—splendid breakers and fine rocks—and he has built a large Grecian house, a nice little church, a conservatory and made excellent gardens and planted numerous trees which look as if they had made up their minds not to grow. However, it is very nice and a very complete place, but alas, Mrs. Cresswell never can enjoy it, for she has wretched health, and spends the greatest part of her time in her room. Her husband, the M.P., is not a bit like his brother; he looks much older, has a long face and greyish hair.

We went to the ball in honour of the Duke of Cornwall[1] last week and I am sorry to say it was a wretched affair—no county people, nothing but townsfolk and not many of them. Consequently it was rather dull, but I did not dislike it and thought it on the whole very good fun. I did not dance, but stood looking on with all my dignity and at 12 we came away. Mrs. Monck and Janetta Ridley were there and Janetta very foolishly went and placed herself next to Matt in the country dance to open the ball. She looked not nice, I must acknowledge. I shook hands with her but did not speak. The Assembly Room[2] is magnificent and there is a little fat Master of the Ceremonies who bustles about and gives an air of importance to the whole affair, but still the honour received by the young Duke was but small at Newcastle.

The more I see of the poor people about here the more I feel puzzled as to the possibility of doing them any good, for they are all so well off. The village of Stannington is the only part that wants improving by gardens and tidiness, and unluckily it belongs to Lord Carlisle whose agent cannot be persuaded to do anything.[3] They all have immense wages and plenty of coal and are quite rich in comparison with our Millbrook people. There is another thing here which

brothers and I imagine that "our Mr. Cresswell" was Sir Cresswell Cresswell, P.C., M.P. for Liverpool and judge of the court of Probate and Divorce.

[1] The Duke of Cornwall, later Prince of Wales and King Edward VII, was born on 9 November 1841.

[2] The Assembly Rooms in Newcastle were built in 1776.

[3] The village of Stannington was bought from the Earl of Carlisle by the first Viscount Ridley in 1900.

makes it rather difficult to do anything and that is the system of
flitting[1] every May, which is done by all the hinds so that they have
no interest in the place and are quite indifferent as to the tidiness
of their cottage. The people belonging to us have all excellent houses
and are very decent and respectable. Your friend Bonomi built the
kennels here and Matt did not consider he behaved quite well in
some respects. However, the kennels are excellent and in beautiful
order.

[1] The custom of flitting is still practised in the North of England,
whereby the hinds or farm labourers change their employer, going from
farm to farm, each May.

CHAPTER SEVEN

Spring 1842

THE Baron and Lady Parke with Mary and Alice spent Christmas at Blagdon, but there is unfortunately no record of their impressions of it or how the party went. On their return to London Cecilia wrote to her mother on 2 January 1842:

So you are really flown and have settled once more in Park Street . . . Dear Mop's funny letter amused me excessively and made me quite rude, for I read it when my guest Mrs. Loraine[1] was in the room and laughed all the time, so that at last I was obliged to apologise and to say that really my sister was so funny I could not help it. Her spirits are not quelled evidently and her fun not gone. Tell her she is quite right about the walks. I went out today with Mrs. Loraine and we were reduced to walking up and down, one after the other, on a narrow slip of hard grass. If we ventured beyond we were either ankle-deep or skating, so we remained plodding on, sheep like, for a short time until Mrs. Loraine declared herself tired and I, being very wet and rather disgusted, came in too, begged her by all means to lie down a little and retired to scribble to you.

She is really rather a pretty looking person and not vulgar or stupid, but she evidently committed a fault in marrying an old, poor husband and I think she seems rather mentally and bodily starved in consequence of that error. However, she walks, not only in silk but in satin attire, and being very poor, keeps on a brand-new gown to walk in the

[1] Mrs. Loraine was the daughter of the Rev. F. Ekins, Rector of Morpeth. She married John Lambton Loraine of Kirkharle, Northumberland, who succeeded to the baronetcy on the death of his brother in 1851 and died the following year aged sixty-seven.

mud with, in spite of my wholesome advice and example. The rest of our guests are all gents with uncommon fine waistcoats. There is Mr. Headlam the doctor's son, who looks as if he was just brought to life again by his father's skill and as if he had very thin poor gruel, instead of blood, in his veins.[1] Mr. Bigge, an officer in the Army and a gent of some pretensions and splendid rings.[2] Captain Burke, one of the moustachioed heroes who were at Ravensworth, and Mr. Fenwick. Today come the Ogles.[3]

I tried very hard last night to make it pleasant, but do not feel satisfied that it was so, although I had my tea table and although I played on the harp, and in short performed all my duties as I best could. The toilet tables would make roast meat of your heart, I am sure, now in the first bloom of their youth and innocence. By the bye, I must tell you that one of the pieces of muslin only had six yards in it. I always do have rain water and have had since you went away, but in spite of that my hands have been immense chapped.

I think the dame you mention seems charming—just the very thing.[4] I suppose I must consult Matt before I think of engaging her. I suppose it will be in about August she would be wanted, but it seems so strange that I can hardly feel sure of it yet. I feel much better than I did a little time ago. In three weeks or less I shall have to go into canny Newcastle for the Assizes and shall stay in the inn, which is very uncanny, but only for two days. It is not worth having a lodging.

[1] Dr. Headlam was a well-known Newcastle physician and one of the original founders of the Medical School of Durham University. He was also actively engaged in local government and politics. He was for many years the most prominent figure in the public life of Newcastle, his influence being said to "resemble that previously held by the Ridleys." Mrs. Headlam was a sister of John Lambton Loraine.

[2] William Bigge, second son of Charles Bigge of Linden, Northumberland. He was in the 66th regiment of native infantry, Bengal.

[3] The Rev. Edward Chaloner Ogle of Kirkley Hall, Ponteland (1798–1853), married in 1830 Sophia, youngest daughter of Admiral Sir Charles Ogle, Bart.

[4] This refers to the engagement of a Nanny.

January 1842 *Blagdon*

Our party is just gone and I think it has been rather dull. There was only Mrs. Ogle and Mrs. Bell at all agreeable and I felt very stupid myself, and this new man Bateman did not manage my tea well, and my harp was out of tune and the lamp would not burn. Mrs. Bell I like rather better on acquaintance but she is not a cultivated person at all. Mrs. Ogle is very much so and I like her extremely.

My doctor is Dr. Dawson,[1] supposed to be the cleverest at Newcastle, Sir John Fife[2] being a surgeon. He has sent me some fresh bottles this morning and thinks I am going on well and there is nothing to be alarmed at. I do not feel strong and am easily upset and flurried, which you saw when you were here. I have taken a great dislike to breakfast, luncheon and dinner, but still I eat enough and I have begun to drink a small glass of beer which seems to suit me. It is charming weather for walking and as there is no hunting I have a nice little walk with Matt every day before luncheon, which is very nice. Today we had a long discussion with a pipe man from Newcastle as to whether the pipes in the vineries should be square or round. The gardener much inclines to the latter owing to his old experience, and the pipe man upholding the former as the ones now universally approved. It ended in our deciding against the gardener, which I fully approved of, as I found that oracle Mr. Mitford had square pipes.

One of the maids has a cough which I am convinced is the whooping cough, although Mrs. Slight maintains that it is not, for the sole reason that she is not a child. I have prescribed for her out of my book —cochineal and tartar. Is there not some other cure you know of?

1842 *Blagdon*

Dearest Papa, I suppose your labours will soon end now, at least those at Liverpool, and I hope you will have a few days to recruit in before

[1] William Dawson, M.D., was Lecturer in Midwifery and senior *accoucheur* to the Lying-In Hospital, Newcastle-upon-Tyne.

[2] Sir John Fife (1795–1871) was a very well-known and distinguished surgeon in Newcastle. Both he and Mr. Dawson were instrumental in forming The College of Medicine and Practical Science in opposition to the Newcastle-upon-Tyne School of Medicine and Surgery. Sir John was also an active radical politician.

C.R.—F

those in London begin. Are you going to try the case of Miss Crellin who was married in her sleep? It seems a very queer concern and I suspect the lady herself is a goose and would be the better for a little chastisement.[1]

We have been going on quietly and peaceably here. The only disputes have been concerning the payment of a clerk. The parish object to the schoolmaster acting in that character as the little boys all begin to fight as soon as he leaves them. And yet the parish object strongly to pay another person and say the vicar ought, and the vicar thinks, on the contrary, that the parish ought. So they have gone on for some time abusing each other and hating each other till the last vestry meeting, when Matt went to preside and restored peace and quiet between them, though not *charity*, I am afraid. I wonder what the law is on the subject? I do not believe the clergyman ever pays the clerk himself. Another deep and great grief is the state of the organ, which positively refuses to play and when it is forced to do so ends with a great shrill squeak which cannot be stopped and much disturbs the devotions of all the congregation.

There has been an affair of honour between the schoolmaster and a ruffian-like blacksmith in the village whose little boy had been punished at school, and who, in consequence, went and abused the master in the most violent language. The affair was represented to the churchwardens who advised the vicar, Mr. Myers, to send for the villain and reprimand him. But the master came and entreated it might not be noticed, as he really could not venture to sleep so near such a ruffian after having offended him so much. So the matter rests.

January 1842   *Blagdon*

Dearest Mama, I have got a pot of salt and am going to use it, but as for having it poured over my back, I do not know how I shall ever

[1] Ann Crellin was abducted from Liverpool by John McGill and "conveyed in a state of perpetual intoxication to Gretna Green where some marriage ceremony was performed", and she woke up to find herself in bed with him next morning. McGill's object was to obtain her fortune of £5,000. He was convicted and sentenced to 18 months hard labour, the jury adding a rider censuring Ann Crellin herself. She preserved her fortune intact, however, if nothing else.

have the courage to let Heseltine into the secrets of my washing; at first, at any rate, I shall content myself with sponging to a great extent. I think it will do me good.

There has been a poor woman nearly dying in her confinement up at the kennels, wife of a kennel servant who is about half her age and uses her shockingly. The poor woman wishes she may die and the man seems to be a wretch, although he looks very decent. They have only been married a short time. Whilst his child was lying dead and his wife supposed to be dying, the man went for the doctor and came home tipsy.

I have not quite decided to have lessons from the Newcastle artist, Mr. Richardson. I think I shall do as well to go on copying and practising. Indeed I rather doubt whether Mr. Thomas Liddell's recommendation would be always safe, he is so enthusiastic and easily excited to admire immensely.[1] However I shall consider it well. Matt was all dismay yesterday at finding I had used half a gallon of his best brandy for my drugs. I drained it through thin muslin and was quite enchanted with my handiwork.

I am puzzled about the nursery. The large upstairs room is the nicest for it, but it will take up such a good spareroom.

January 1842   *Blagdon*

Dearest Mama, Thank you for your nice dear letter. How delightful it would be if all mothers were like you, and what a world of troubles would have been avoided thereby. I think I see now pretty well what Lady Ridley is and begin to understand her. Very selfish and with the highest possible opinion of her own merits compared with those of the rest of the world. I am not so afraid of her as I was, but still I wish she was not to be in town when we are there. I always feel strongly inclined to talk about the school etc. when I write to her, but perhaps it is better not. I think when you see her again it would be as well if you said something about my *prospects*, for she knows about it and she might perhaps otherwise say of you, as she did of her son George, how unfeeling it was not to talk to her of what you knew must give her pleasure. What a bore she is!

[1] The Hon. Thomas Liddell, second son of Lord Ravensworth.

I must tell you that I have the housebooks all my own way now and Matt does not even look at them. I think he is kinder about Mrs. Cookson than he was before. She talked to me the other day about Henry and said exactly what Matt does—that he never will take advice or conciliate anybody and that he cannot resist buying anything he fancies.

Think of Slight seriously proposing to me to keep a man baker. Did you ever hear such nonsense?

January 1842 *Blagdon*

Many thanks for all the trouble you have taken for me. Miss T. sent down all the baby clothes yesterday and Heseltine looked at them and said "Well, we must not take a pattern from *them*, my Lady," so I suppose she is prepared for the occupation that awaits her.

This fine weather suits me much and I get nice quiet strolls about the place that do me a world of good. The quiet, regular life we lead too is very wholesome and we shall be but little interrupted till we go south. A few days of Assizes and a day or two at Mitford, but very likely no more company at home, at least I hope not, for I do not like it. It is very stupid only having neighbours to meet each other, but one cannot help it in these Northern climes. The Mitfords called here the other day and she chattered dreadfully at the end of her tongue and was very full of gossip.[1] I really do not fancy her. Mrs. Ogle suits me far better and is really a pleasant companion. The single gentlemen who come here I really cannot abide, at least I do not admire them. Mr. James, last time he was here, was so very queer, so mysterious and so odd that I thought he must have exceeded a little. However I found out it was his usual way of talking.

February 1842 *Blagdon*

I think you will say that I am a very variable, inconstant dame, always changing my pursuit. I told you I had got the key of the beetle case in my room[2] and there I saw unfolded to my view a very

[1] Robert Mitford, of Mitford Hall near Morpeth, married in 1830 Margaret, daughter of James Dunsmure, of Edinburgh.

[2] This beetle case is still at Blagdon.

charming collection and not a very small one, all crowded together and no names. So I routed out all the books in the library concerning beetles and set about trying to find out something about them, which was very difficult as there is no good book on the subject here. However, I made out a few and got pretty well acquainted with them and I shall try and get some better book from the museum at Newcastle. . . . I have at last got Warren Hastings and we are reading him aloud in the evenings.[1] I was quite sorry not to go on with him yesterday (Sunday) and I am afraid that Matt will be somewhat too sleepy for it after his hunting today.

Yesterday we had a Mr. Romney to dine and sleep—a young clergyman just come into the neighbourhood and lodging in an antiquated farmhouse three miles from his village and quite inaccessible to carriage. He is a quiet little man and seems sensible and right minded. But Oh! it was hard work "making the agreeable" to him. Matt had some letters to answer which took a little time and Henry sat in apathy and indifference. I pumped and pumped till I thought I must have taken the poker to them and given them both a good beating. At last when Matt had done we got on rather better, till Henry chose to begin a great discussion about Newmanism, which he delights in and which provokes me beyond all measure. I am convinced he knows nothing about it, but he will talk and he likes a discussion. He is a most provoking creature. Only think what he is going to do: his old landlady is leaving the house, so he has set up for himself. Being at present in debt one would think he would try and economise. Not a bit. He says his room is not cheerful, he must make two new windows in it besides the two there are, must alter the garden, buy all the furniture of all the rooms instead of doing with one, and in short live in style. He has been away from home every week lately for four or five days, goes again tomorrow, and then next Monday for his three weeks in town. And to make up the measure of his iniquities he is perpetually buying all sorts of books and told me only yesterday he

[1] *Memoirs of the Life of Warren Hastings, first Governor-General of Bengal.* Compiled from Original Papers by the Rev. G. R. Gleig, M.A. (3 vols., 1841). Macaulay's famous review appeared in the *Edinburgh Review* for October 1841.

had bought the new Oxford prayer book and sent it to town to have a clasp put to it, just as if he had thousands instead of hundreds a year. Is it not silly of him and tiresome?

I went this morning to see the butter made and stood by to see that the dairymaid beat it properly. She did not do it half enough, I thought, and seemed quite to disagree with my view of the case, so I am going to see Mrs. Gibson make hers and then, if I find I am right, and if I cannot make the maid do as I like, she shall go. I have to inform you that we shall not go to town till quite the end of April or perhaps the first week in May.

February 1842. *Blagdon*

I did not write yesterday for various reasons, one of which was that I thought the roads were so blocked my letter would not go, which I believe was the case. We have shut out the saloon, little drawing room and dining room and live in great comfort and snuggitude in the hall and library. But really today was shocking. Never did I see anything so dark, so windy, so snowy, so sleety as it has been. This evening everything was thawing but I imagine it was only what they call a sea fret and that we shall see frost and snow again tomorrow.

Lady Ridley has popped off to Brighton, to our immense surprise. What her secret motives may be I cannot divine, except it be to get away from her son George. I am glad, at least I shall be if she stays long, for it would be a relief to you not to have her in town when you first go. She spoke very affectionately of you all.

We are by degrees getting the books arranged, which is a great comfort. But I am very good and do very little of that sort with my own hands, lie down constantly, and in short "take mine ease in mine Inn."[1] Mrs. Slight and I are at daggers drawn about butter. I was quite angry with her about it. I spoke with great earnestness about working it properly and she said "Very well, we can do it but we always think it makes the butter soft and bad." I think it will end in my dispatching the dairymaid, old as she is and piercing as are her eyes, for I see very well she is good for 0.

Tell dear Mary that I read a *Märchen* of Novalis today till I felt

[1] Shakespeare: *Henry IV, Part I.*

my senses gradually going and it was all so wild and queer. It is one told by KLINGSOHR, all about the stars dancing in a room and ladies floating through seas of ice and little boys waking with silver wings. It is most unfathomable. I am very crazy in consequence.

[Sir Matthew was High Sheriff for Northumberland in 1842, and he and Cecilia stayed at the Queen's Head Hotel in Newcastle for the February Assizes. The judges were Sir W. Whiteman and Mr. Justice Rolfe. Cecilia wrote to her mother from there on 26 February:]

Here I am in canny Newcastle, established in a very nice, quiet cheerful room in the celebrated Hotel of Her Majesty's Head, with a fine view into the splendid street below and my cold being in the act of departing. Matt came in here yesterday morning and I followed in the afternoon, having in the meanwhile had two hearty luncheons, one at twelve and the other at three. Yesterday we had Messrs. Donkin and Staple to dine, the attorneys who do the Ridley business. One a fat old man, the exact image of Miss Hurst. The other pale and thin and sickly, something like the Duke of Bedford. We had the Sheriff's footman to wait, who looked so magnificent in the small room that I felt as if he was degrading himself by waiting upon us. The dinner went off capitally, and afterwards I had an interview with the manager of the theatre, settled about my "bespeak," and then gave a discourse on the subject of tea to the waiter. In consequence of which we had a delicious repast and such a silver teapot and such a kettle, so boiling, all very comfortable. Our two friends were very agreeable. "Miss Hurst" is great on the subject of camellias and has treated himself to a splendid work on the subject which he sent me this morning. He has also given £240 for a work on American birds which he insists upon making a box for and sending it out to me at Blagdon.[1] He is Under Sheriff and looks very well with a great sword by his side.

Oh dear, how uncomfortable my bed was last night. Such a slope from the head to the foot and the clothes so narrow they kept slipping off and I kept slipping down and it was very provoking. However, never mind, it is past. I have this morning dispatched a haunch of

[1] Audubon's *Birds of America*, consisting of 435 coloured plates, was published in 1838.

venison and cream cheese to the judges, my worthy uncles, also a basket of flowers which I brought in on purpose for Mr. Dundas. I have also seen a great sight: the High Sheriff in his full dress. Oh that I should have survived it! The like these eyes never before rested on, and never will after these Assizes. Seriously, he looked very nice. I watched the judges going past and wished Papa was there, but even as it was, I felt quite pleased to see them and as if I belonged to them, almost. I am going into court today for a little while, play tonight, Mr. Dundas tomorrow, ball Monday.

1 March 1842   *Blagdon*

I have returned to the quiet shades of Blagdon and cast off the title of Mrs. High for ever. Yesterday was the ball and I thought it very pleasant and enjoyable, although thin. Lady Ravensworth came and told me she had come on purpose to see me. She was very kind to me and made me go and sit by her for some time, but she went away early, as Lord Ravensworth was very unwell.[1] Miss Liddell was there, very smart, fresh from the Queen, with divers pretty, shining *cadeaux* about her, and Mr. Augustus was there too. They will probably go South sooner than they intended owing to Lord Ravensworth's indisposition. Sir E. and Lady Blackett[2] were there, so I went and sat by her and she was very nice, but did not look so pretty as I had thought her. She called upon me this morning before I came

[1] Sir Thomas Henry Liddell was created Baron Ravensworth in 1821, re-creating the title that had become extinct at the death of his uncle, from whom he inherited the estates of Ravensworth in Co. Durham and Eslington in Northumberland. He built a magnificent castle at Ravensworth to the designs of Nash, which was pulled down in the 1930's. The family still live at Eslington. Lady Ravensworth was a Miss Simpson of Bradley Hall, Co. Durham. They had eight sons and eight daughters, the youngest of whom, Georgina, afterwards Lady Bloomfield, was born when her mother was fifty-one. George IV is said to have bet her £5 that she would not have a baby after the age of fifty. Georgina was at this time Maid of Honour to Queen Victoria. Augustus Liddell was the twelfth child and sixth son.

[2] Sir Edward Blackett (1805–85) was in the Life Guards. He married in 1830 Julia, daughter of Sir Charles Monck of Belsay. Sir Edward built a large mansion at Matfen, Northumberland.

away. I saw no lawyers at the ball, plenty of Cooksons, Bells, etc., but not a single pretty person. We came away at twelve, being ordered by the inflexible "Wag" to be early again this morning, so there was no fatigue.

I took our own tea to the inn and we had cream in a bottle sent out from Blagdon, which was a great comfort, for our cream is really good now.

5 March 1842   *Blagdon*
Dearest Papa, . . . The hunting season is fast drawing to a close and has been a very unfortunate one on the whole. There was such a long stoppage and since then the scents have been so bad, indeed they have killed so few foxes, that I am afraid it will be a sad time for the chickens and there will be a dearth of poultry throughout the land. It is a great comfort to find a dry place for the sole of one's foot and I quite rejoice in being able to walk about anywhere now with comfort. When it is not a hunting day I explore the fields and woods with Matt and make acquaintance with our possessions. But when I am alone I generally confine myself to walks nearer home and spend a great deal of time in poddling about the garden and making little arrangements therein.

The great affair going on at present is brewing, and now that Emperor Priddle shines forth in all his glory, there is heard by cockcrow each morning a great sound of a rolling about of barrels and hammering of casks and chattering of tongues. And there is seen, if I chance to cast my eyes that way, a great sight in the shape of a huge round grinning man, a perfect model for a Falstaff, who comes here at this season to act as Secretary of State for brewing affairs to Emperor Priddle. Whether the said Emperor condescends to lend a helping hand himself, I cannot say, or whether he merely watches over the proceedings with his royal eye, but certainly somehow or other the brew continues to be a successful affair and it is no joke. The harvest people alone drank 380 gallons last year.

You seem to be much more gaily disposed than your brothers Mousey and Wag.[1] Nothing would induce them to stir out at night.

[1] Nicknames for Baron Rolfe and Sir W. Whiteman.

In vain we implored them to come to the ball and offered them seats in our box at the theatre. They said they had resolved to give up balls on the circuit, and the bar seemed to have followed their example, for I did not see a single lawyer I knew at the ball. In court I saw a few old friends, but very few, and I must say it struck me that the barristers were a very snobby, shabby, sloppy looking set compared with what they were when I last went the circuit at York.

I have been today to see Mrs. Riddell, mother of the present High Sheriff, a very nice *stiffish* old Catholic lady.[1] There is a Miss Riddell too, who seems to me very much to be commended and I hope I shall see more of them. They seem quite amongst the nicest of our neighbours. I have got such sweet lilies of the valley. I wish I could send you some.

March 1842   *Blagdon*

I made an expedition to Newcastle yesterday and enjoyed myself very much. I will tell you what we did. First we did a little business: Matt signed away his Shrievalty and we had a little shopping, and then we paid a visit to a certain Mrs. Dixon, a good lady with a sort of *latitude* and *beatitude* countenance who was sitting in a very tidy, very hot room with two old spins as companions, squinny old ladies that looked as if the word squinny was invented for them. We had luncheon with these fat and thin pink-faced, yellow-faced dames and then walked on to Mr. Adamson's, where Matt had some slight business and I thought I might sit down and wait for him. But behold, we were asked into a drawing room full of curiosities and books and work and comforts, and graced by the presence of a large, fat old lady in a flaxen wig, who proved to be Mrs. Adamson to my infinite surprise. Then came a daughter, then a son, and at last Mr. Adamson himself, who was delighted to see me and immediately drew forth his keys, unlocked his cabinets and did the honours.

[1] Mrs. Riddell, wife of Ralph Riddell of Felton and Swinburne Castle, Northumberland, was the daughter of Joseph Blount of Mapledurham. Her husband died in 1833. Her son Thomas married the daughter of William Throckmorton in 1827.

I have been rather idle about writing these few last days. The fact is I have had nothing to tell you but the same things repeated again and nothing remarkable has occurred. I see a trouble appearing, however, for I find George Ridley is already in the neighbourhood and William coming this week. I now almost despair of their being asked here, which of course will make matters worse, but I will not quite despair yet. Henry is rather better than before and much occupied with pruning his fruit trees in his garden which he seems to enjoy.

Mr. Myers is an old humbug. He has never for years attended the vestry meeting, which is very wrong, and this year it happened that he had to go to the funeral of a friend that day. So he made many apologies and expressed great sorrow and annoyance at not being able to attend the said meeting. There is not a creature in the parish that can endure him. And yet the old man has a kind heart at bottom. Yesterday he chose to preach about people not going to church and abused all ranks right and left for their shameful negligence. Now it happened that these three last Sundays there has been a great increase of numbers at church and really a fair attendance on the whole. And as for the higher ranks that he abused, there are none in the parish but us and we do not deserve such a scold. About four men and eight maids of ours go now, and Bateman sometimes, but he has a cough. The stable men really cannot go, even coaching, for there is no place for them to put up the horses near the church.

We always have a walk after church, then Matt brings me home and takes another walk, and then he comes up to my room and reads the Bible to me, and then come dinner and Henry together.

CHAPTER EIGHT

Little Matt

THERE is a gap in the letters for the summer of 1842, when Matt and Cecilia were in London and she was presumably seeing her mother every day. In July her sister Mary became engaged to Charles Howard, fifth son of the sixth Earl of Carlisle, and on 25 July Cecilia's baby Matthew White was born at 10 Carlton House Terrace. Cecilia refers to both these events in a letter to Aunt Fanny written some time in August 1842:

Dearest Aunt Fanny, I am very anxious to write and tell you all about your little nephew, and also to thank you for the little socks you sent which I hope will prove very acceptable to some little feet before very long. I am quite pleased with my brother [-in-law]. He is a dear creature that no one can help loving. So warm-hearted, so open, so good, so unselfish, in short so full of all the qualities most necessary to ensure dear Mary's happiness. He is not handsome, but really I begin now to admire his face. He looks so good and improves so upon acquaintance. Then his family are all so charming. Such a good, tender mother, and such a little pet of a sister, and all the married ones so united and so affectionate. They are all, with one accord, disposed to welcome Mary with all possible cordiality, and I feel no doubt at all that she has decided much to her happiness and will have one of the best of husbands. She is perfectly calm and composed about it all and quite surprises me by the little agitation she shows. Mama, too, seems quite at ease on the subject, and to have no doubt that Mary had done wisely. Charles Howard seems an especial favourite with all his family and to have a great number of true and good friends.

[She wrote to her mother about the same time:]

10 Carlton House Terrace

I suppose you know that Mary is returned from her wanderings. They dined here yesterday and Charles dozed and Mary pinched him. Except during that time he was very agreeable and very nice and very charming. The dear baby is so well and getting on so nicely now. It is quite delightful, and most thankful indeed am I that it is so. He had his first walk yesterday, put on his lovely little hood and his new cloak and looked such a darling. He was wide awake all the time and much struck by the trees and also by a Punch and Judy that was going by. As for me, I am quite well and walk about as if nothing had happened. I am also become a most excellent nurse, in spite of which I am sorely tormented by that busybody Mrs. Malloch because I do not devour as much as Lady Hastings, and this morning I had no sooner finished my breakfast when she appeared bearing sandwiches and beer, which she nearly forced down my throat, but luckily I had Nurse to help me, so I escaped. . . . Nurse said she must have ten guineas, which was her usual price in the country even, and she did not think it fair towards London nurses to take so much less than they. However as soon as the doctor had gone she repented and thought it was behaving ill to you and sent to say she would take doctor's terms. She is a nice, good, excellent woman and so sensible about everything. She quite surprises me by her conversation . . . I asked Dr. Lowick when we might go and he said by the middle of next week, but when I said we were going straight home he seemed to think the journey too long, so we have not settled yet.

[Evidently they did go, as the next letter is postmarked Grantham:]

You would like to hear how the darling is. He has slept nearly all the way and looks better but is not yet free from that tiresome complaint. I think the journey is rather trying in that respect as it makes him so irregular in his hours. I hope when he is settled at Blagdon he will improve more and more. If he continues at all unwell I shall feel convinced it must be owing to me and give up nursing him. I cannot help thinking it is so, though the doctor at last assured me not. We have had a very comfortable journey and are safely lodged at Grantham. The day's journey is quite enough for me. I find such a pain in my back after it, and yet it is a very comfortable carriage and I have a board between the seats. I shall say goodbye and go to bed now. I hear all the landladies admire Baby very much.

September 1842   *Blagdon*

We are just arrived at home and the place looks so nice I was quite surprised—so green and fresh and cheerful you would not know it. Dear Baby is established in his new nursery and is laughing and looking quite happy. He is so much better now that I have no doubt that he will now thrive and that I may go on nursing with confidence and without fears of not doing right by the little darling.

I must tell you all the adventures of our journey. At Doncaster we had a visit from Aunt Marianne who was in high beauty and great spirits. She was very mysterious about her visit—pretended to have some business in the town and engagements to tea and to sleep at somebody's house, and it was not till she was going away in the evening when we wanted to get her cloak that we discovered that she was in the next room to us in the inn. I took her a brown gown. I hope she liked it.

The next day was full of troubles. First of all it rained and poured. Then I was in a great hurry to get to York early and *so* one of our horses turned out so weak that we were obliged to stop and have one sent to meet us from Selby. Then at York, having five servants, we did not like to invade Grandmama's house. So we left them at the Inn with directions for Nurse to feed Baby and bring him on immediately. However they all made mistakes and he was not fed but came on ravenous to Bootham, which put all the house in a commotion to get his food made, and made us so late that we did not get to Northallerton till near eight, all in the rain. It was very foolish not taking Baby at once to Bootham, but it was all done with the idea of having a quiet visit there and not putting all the house in a fuss. Aunt Fanny was hardly to be satisfied without my eating apricots and apple tart and thought we might have staid much longer, but I got very fidgetty, for I thought it so bad for Baby to be out late. He was taken up to Grandmama, who gave him her blessing in bed. Poor old lady, I thought she seemed altered but I was only allowed a peep. Nurse was terribly put out about the mistake and I saw her temper appear visibly for the first time. She did not recover till the next day. It was not her fault however.

Northallerton was very comfortable, barring a smell of tobacco, and we have had a very peaceful, pleasant journey today. Very fine and bright, no mistakes, no tired horses, no rain. My little nurserymaid looks quite a pet. I am afraid the footmen will fall in love with her. Do you think I had better let Wells have any medicines etc. to keep for Baby or keep them all myself?

I have got my good eyes on today, I think, for Blagdon seems to me twice as nice as before, and certainly the improvement in a certain passage beyond my dressing room is wonderful.[1] Poor Mrs. Slight seems like an angel after that black contrast in London. She was quite nervous at seeing Baby, quite affected by it. I must tell you that I am certainly gaining courage, for I actually had the boldness to tell the landlady at Grantham that she had given us a vile breakfast.

The garden looketh not pretty. Grey has exercised his wretched taste in colours and has made blue and lilac abound in a very unpleasant manner . . . We were asked to meet H.R.H. of Cambridge at Alnwick but of course I say No.

September 1842   *Blagdon*

Dearest Mama, I am quite behindhand with my news for you, for really I find that with proper attention to both Baby and my guests I have not much time to spare. Wonders will never cease. I like my Aunt Catherine [Ridley] exceedingly. Indeed I am charmed with her and quite astonished that I *am* charmed. I understand her manner now and I see that I was quite wrong in thinking that her grave looks meant displeasure. She has a great deal of fun in her and is an

---

[1] This passage was in the nursery wing built by Cecilia's mother-in-law. It was called "The Nunnery" as it was occupied by her daughters. When they left home Lady Ridley had their bedroom doors bricked up. Perhaps Cecilia had reopened them.

excellent, honest, straightforward creature, though certainly unlike the rest of the world. As for him, he is not wise but very good and so fond of this place and full of recollections and associations with everything—every picture and every room—that he is quite agreeable. I think it really gives an interest to the place to see him here, with all his boyish recollections.

Now for the christening. You know Matt wished to have it on our wedding day, and we thought old Mr. Burrell[1] was so very infirm he would not be able to walk to the church. Besides which we had some slight fears as to Baby in that cold damp place. So, much against my conscience and my wish, we settled to have it in the house. However, on Sunday, Mr. Bastard preached against the practice of baptising in houses—very strongly too—so that we felt quite ashamed of ourselves. And then we found there was a difficulty about another person performing the ceremony in his parish, so we decided to have it on Thursday in the church. Mr. Burrell was only to come in the afternoon on Wednesday, and accordingly it took place there, and most heartily glad am I that we did so settle it, for I think it was much more satisfactory and right, both for our own sakes and as an example, particularly as the Archdeacon has been anxious to discourage the private baptism. Baby was very good indeed and only gave one little squeak. Mr. Burrell got to church very well and it was not cold and everyone was delighted it should be there instead of in the house. Baby was brought down in the evening, clad, for the first and last time in his life, in white satin, and looked beautiful. Mrs. Ridley represented Lady Ridley and Mr. Burrell Papa. That old man was full of anecdotes of old times which he tells very well. He has a good memory and a very kind heart, and he is full of the milk of human kindness and ready to do anything to help a friend. I never saw a nicer old gentleman than he is, with his enormous red face and purple nose. Henry Ridley is here now and does not look lovely. I think he has got rather spoiled by being made much of amongst the Bigges at Felton. My striped gown looks very well and sticks out beautifully.

[1] William Burrell (1773–1847) of Broome Park, Edlingham, Northumberland.

September 1842   *Blagdon*

Mr. Bastard, the curate, dined here yesterday. He is a very *pleasant* person, very cheerful and sensible and good. I like him much and think he will do perhaps better than Henry, being more steady. You will be surprised to hear that my flower garden has really been admired. Indeed, it does look decent, strange to say . . . The Duke of Cambridge[1] was in Newcastle on Saturday and overwhelmed the Mayor and Corporation with questions respecting the town—none of which they were able to answer.

All the maids came up to see Baby in his christening robe. All the people about are very anxious to see him; indeed, many of the old women want to kiss him, which I am obliged to forbid. I went to see a woman just confined in one of the cottages and found her baby in a cape trimmed with lace and its cuffs tied with white satin, much smarter than Baby was the first month.

October 1842   *Blagdon*

Dearest Papa, I must write you a few lines to wish you joy of your employment. I hope you will be free from gout and toothache and be able to go back to pheasant-shooting at Ampthill. Mrs. Ridley, who abounds in sovereign remedies, has, amongst others, one for the gout which she said she would send you. She described its wonderful effects on her father, as making the attacks much less severe and the pain less intense. But I found he was past 80, so that I thought that it might have been old age and not the medicine that had the effect. Mrs. Ridley had also a cure for consumption which she administered to poor Bateman, but I fear it will do very little for him.

Baby and I are left to entertain each other now, which we do very well. He is grown a great darling and I often wish you and Mama could see him when he is lying on his nurse's lap laughing and crowing and kicking about his little fat legs. Sir John Fife came last week

[1] When H.R.H. The Duke of Cambridge visited Tyneside he stayed with Lord Ravensworth, who "brought his Royal guest to Newcastle, showed him all the sights of the town, including the Exhibition of the North East Fine Arts Society, and piloted him through the tedium of receiving addresses from the Corporations of Newcastle and Gateshead".

to vaccinate him and made many enquiries after you. He seemed to approve of colchicum when properly combined, and said there was no foundation for all the prejudices people have against it.

That good old gentleman of the old school, Mr. Burrell was found to stand for you as Godfather and was rejoicing to hear of you going on the Special Commission. He came to see me the other day with his wife who has a *burr* surpassing all *burrs* I have heard yet. Only think of the Duke of Cambridge passing so many days in the county without my catching a glimpse of his royal person. He behaved very unhandsomely at Alnwick, where there was a large house party invited to meet him, for he was enticed away by the Liddells and went off to the Festival, leaving all the party in the lurch.[1] The last thing that I heard of him was that at Wynyard[2] he chose to take in a pretty young lady instead of Lady Londonderry, and on being told of his mistake by the Marquess he said it was the best mistake he could make and went on, to the great dismay of the noble hostess.

I like our new curate much. He remembers you at Cambridge when you had the lumbago, and says that before you arrived there a set of mischievous men had gone into your rooms and taken every bit of furniture and thrown it all into the river, out of which it was dragged, but the beds not much the better for the wetting. The said Mr. Bastard is a very large fat young man and is obliged to walk sixteen miles a day to keep himself in health. He is a great gardener and very fond of good ale and explained to us with great clearness the difference between stout and porter, which I always before thought were the same thing. He told us too of the system of *espionage* carried on by the great brewers, who send out men to all the public houses that belong to them to ask for a pint of porter, which is then brought to them and examined and if found to be weakened the man of the public house loses his place. The spies are constantly changed and sent about in different dresses so that they never can be known.

[1] A "Grand Musical Festival" was held on 27 September 1842 in St. Nicholas Church, Newcastle, for the benefit of charity.

[2] Wynyard Park, near Stockton-on-Tees, belongs to the Marquess of Londonderry.

October 1842   *Blagdon*

Dearest Mama, Mrs Slight had thirty guineas which I do not think much for a good housekeeper, do you? I am sure she is an excellent woman and I think she was a good housekeeper as far as the management of the servants went, though not particularly so in little *niceties*. She was so regular and methodical and her manner with the servants so good.

I had a long visit today from Sarah Cookson and her piccaninny. I heard from her that the Duke of Cambridge, when seated at the end of the room at Wynyard between Lady Barrington and Lady Londonderry, exclaimed "There is one young lady who ought to be here and is not and I cannot tell why, and that is Lady Ridley. Why is she not here?" "I am sure I do not know," says Lady Barrington, and after some time, when people thought it was all forgotten, he said "I knew there was a reason but I could not recollect and now I know—she is nursing her baby, Lady Parke told me so." Was not that funny? Also I have learned what before was a mystery to me, why the Richard Ridleys never came here but once since old Sir Matthew Ridley's death twenty-nine years ago. Matt and Lady Ridley had always told me that they were invited and pressed to come every year, and yet Mrs. Ridley spoke of it as if they had never had an opportunity given them, and the truth was that they never were allowed to see the children except by stealth, and consequently they said they never would come again as long as Lady Ridley was here. The children were never allowed to come into the room, and one day Mr. Ridley was caught with the baby in his arms, which caused great anger. Yet Mrs. Ridley spoke with much affection of Lady Ridley. I suppose she sees some redeeming points, though she sees her faults too.

I must tell you what I think very odd, but do not say anything to anybody about it. Mrs. Malloch told me, the night I was confined, that she knew what it was, for she had suffered in the same way. Today I asked Heseltine whether Mrs. Malloch had ever been married and she said No, that she often talked about it and said she should die an old maid. Is not that odd?

I am going to make myself as smart as possible for the Ravensworth Fête. Everybody is going in white muslin and I shall go in that muslin with the wavy coral stripe and have some of my wedding lace twiddled into a cardinal. The house is to be all shut in and lighted up so one need not be wrapped up, and Mrs. Thomas Liddell begs every one will be smart. Goodbye, dearest Mama, how nice it would have been to have had you with me.

[This fête was held at Ravensworth Castle on 8 October 1842, in honour of the coming of age of Henry George Liddell, eldest son of the Hon. Henry Thomas Liddell, eldest son of Lord Ravensworth. I have been unable to discover the significance of everyone being asked to wear white and cherry colour, but it must have made the party very pretty.]

9 October 1842   *Blagdon*

I found your letter when I returned from Ravensworth last night and am now going to tell you all about the eventful day, which went off, as everything arranged by the Liddells does, exceedingly well. All Northumberland and Durham were there and some of London besides, to the number, I should think, of five hundred or more. We arrived there about five and were ushered into the long gallery and greeted most affectionately by Lady Barrington, Lady Williamson, Lady Normanby, Lady Hardwicke, and Miss Liddell,[1] all dressed in white muslin trimmed in divers ways with cherry-coloured ribbon and all preparing to sing. Lady Normanby took me by the arm and dragged me along, exclaiming that I must have a good place to hear the music, and consigned me to Lord Normanby's care, who placed me in the centre of the room where I saw and heard beautifully. The organ was played by the Newcastle organist and all the sisters stood before it in a half circle with the brothers and sang the Hallelujah Chorus and other sacred pieces, ending with God Save the Queen. The effect was splendid. The gallery was, all the time, perfectly *crammed* so full of people, only a little place in the centre, where sat H.R.H. of Gloucester[2] and Lady Ravensworth, and where stood I, surrounded by Lady Prudhoe,[1] Miss Percy, etc., and making myself very

[1] Five of the eight daughters of Lord and Lady Ravensworth.

[2] Princess Mary, daughter of George III, married her first cousin, the Duke of Gloucester.

agreeable to all. Of course the Royal Duchess was graciously pleased to come and talk to me a good deal, and I, being unaccustomed to addressing Royalty, was rather puzzled. Lady Ravensworth was most kind to me and seemed bent on taking a motherly care of me. I made acquaintance with Lady Prudhoe, who, by the bye, looked rather dowdy. She had on her wedding dress which was very *skimpy*, and a blue silk bonnet with a long veil (not a *voilette*) hanging on one side, and looking, as I have seen often, when people have just come out of a coach or a steam packet, like a long white rag. Lord Prudhoe was as blithe as a bee and quite youthful. To return to my history of the day—the music being over we all stood still for some time, unable to move in any direction, till there was a cry of dinner, very agreeable to all, and then we all rushed on as best we could. Mr. Silvertop[2] was close to me and very anxious to follow the *big wigs* and get a place amongst them, but he was, like us, disappointed and obliged to wait till the first set had finished. Dinner was in the library for the Royal party and in the drawing room and dining room for all the rest. Two narrow tables in each room—the whole length. Lord Hardwick gave all the toasts from the library and they were repeated in the drawing room by Mr. George Liddell, and in the dining room by another brother, which was very gay and well managed. About half past seven dinner was over and then all the ladies went upstairs and there took

[1] Lady Eleanor Grosvenor, daughter of the Marquess of Westminster, married in August 1842 Algernon, Baron Prudhoe (1792–1865), brother of the third Duke of Northumberland. He had a distinguished career in the Navy, being promoted to the rank of Commander. In 1852 he became the first First Lord of the Admiralty. He was also a scholar and archaeologist, accompanying Sir John Herschel on his astronomical survey to the Cape of Good Hope, when he collected many valuable Egyptian relics, which are now in the British Museum and Durham University. He also organised an extensive survey of the ancient Roman and British forts and roads in Northumberland, but he himself considered his greatest claim to fame to have been his restoration of Alnwick Castle after he succeeded his brother as fourth Duke in 1847.

[2] George Silvertop of Minsteracres, Co. Durham, visited Napoleon while he was on Elba, and Napoleon subsequently told Dr. O'Meara that it was the conversation he had had with Silvertop that largely persuaded him to make the attempt to regain power during the Hundred Days.

off their bonnets and combed their hair, after which they came down into the gallery and dancing began. There were to be fireworks but as we came away at eight we did not see them. There was tea at the end of the room, made most admirably by that praiseworthy maid of Lady Ravensworth's, clad in white and cherry colour. I must say a word in praise of her and all the other maids: they were so attentive and so active and did everything so well. It was really beautiful to see all the numerous Liddell family assembled with their smiling, happy faces. There were all the daughters except Mrs. Trotter and Mrs. Villiers, all the sons and all their wives, and many grandchildren besides, a beautiful Miss Barrington amongst others. My dress did very well and my bonnet was twiddled with some of my Mechlin lace in a wonderful way. Heseltine said she wished you could see it. There was a large man in regimentals who came and scraped his epaulettes along my back, thereby making an immense rent in my elegant cardinal, upon which I looked round and—like Mr. Rogers—showed him the human face divine and felt inclined to beat him. But with that exception I enjoyed myself excessively. I knew so many people and they were all so kind and civil and I was in good spirits and never liked anything better. I had had quite enough when I came away, for it was very tiring. There were some Austrian Archdukes, concerning whom Lord Normanby made a long speech which nobody could hear.[1] Lady Mary Monck[2] took her maid and twiddled herself out with all sorts of fine things. The Brandlings[3] were in crimson velvet robes given by the Duchess of R. with sleeves done round in a corkscrew way with lace—not at all pretty, for their arms looked like bolsters.

I saw nothing to copy, for all were in white muslins and cardinals. I thought *I* looked very well. The Duchess of Northumberland was

[1] Archduke Frederick Ferdinand Leopold of Austria (1821–47) was at the Ravensworth fête with his suite. I can find no evidence that any other Archdukes were present, though Lord Normanby, who proposed the heath of Archduke Ferdinand, Emperor of Austria, may well have spoken of them.

[2] Lady Mary Bennett, daughter of the fourth Earl of Tankerville, married Sir Charles Monck of Belsay Castle, Northumberland.

[3] Of Gosforth Park, near Newcastle. The house is now the grandstand of the Newcastle race-course.

not there, having lost a friend lately. The party was kept up till three.

17 October 1842 *Blagdon*

I want to ask your advice on an important subject—that is, whether under all the circumstances it is expedient for me to go on nursing Baby. He requires so much feeding now. Today he has been fed three times besides the night, and after he has been with me he scarcely ever seems quite satisfied now. He is almost always sick, more so after being nursed than after being fed. Still he thrives very well, his interior is quite right and he seems perfectly well. What do you think of the matter? As for myself, I am very well. It is not on that account I was at all thinking of giving him up, but merely because Wells said that it would be better to wean him now than whilst teething was going on. So will you tell me what you think. I have no pain in my back now and can walk almost as much as before.

I have done 0 to my table covers. One is not begun but the wool is wound for it, the other has about an inch finished. . . . Poor Bateman looks like a ghost: it is dreadful to see him and more so to hear him speak.

Lady Ridley has sent Baby a beautiful coral set in engraved gold with two little gold bells and the crest engraved on it. It is really a beautiful thing and Baby has it hung round his waist and plays with it. I hope Papa will not distress himself about giving Baby a present. He had much better not. The Rev. Richard came empty-handed. I was rather sorry he went only to Linden from here, as I meant to have heaped coals of fire on his head by giving him an excellent luncheon in the carriage.[1]

Dearest Mama, I have to thank you for your long letter of advice and counsel. I am rather puzzled how best to act, for I think I should be afraid to give up nursing him unless I got a wet nurse after what you say, and as he is so well I think I had better go on as well as I can, a little. I cannot get any opinion from Wells: she is so funny one can never tell what she thinks.

[1] Linden is only ten miles from Blagdon. Cecilia is referring to the fact that the Richard Ridleys only gave her sponge biscuits to eat when she stayed with them the year before, on the way home from her honeymoon.

CHAPTER NINE

Autumn 1842

TOWARDS the end of October 1842 Mary and her husband Charles Howard stayed at Blagdon, which gave Cecilia immense joy. She wrote to her mother:

I have been waiting to write to you till I could tell you all about dear Mary. She came here on Saturday and is blooming and full of fun and spirits and seems as happy as possible. We had such a nice morning today cleaning our colour boxes like old times. She has made some such nice sketches, much improved I think. . . . She has mopsied a pair of boots, a penknife, a cake of colour, a blue handkerchief, some books and the pole of the Brougham!

[And a day or two later:]

Mary is in immense spirits and very blooming. She is always laughing and Charles laughing in sympathy. She never walks across the room without making a *cheese* or some funny vagary. Her sketches are really charming, particularly the grey paper ones. I never saw any better and she does them so easily without any parade at all.

We have had some charming mornings, Charles reading aloud to us whilst we worked or drew in my little room, for the weather has not allowed us to go out much. Yesterday we went to Newcastle and Mary made many purchases, a plaid gown and velvet for a cap for Charles. She was very funny, seemed quite afraid of asking for anything or speaking to the shopman and made me ask for her. Was it not funny of her? We went to see a curious thing—the Grand Centrifugal Railroad. We saw it written up as we walked along the street

MARY HOWARD
A SELF-PORTRAIT

and popped in to see what manner of thing it was. We were told at
the door we might either pay sixpence or a shilling. I daresay you
can guess which we chose. It is a little carriage which comes with
great force down an inclined plane, round the inside of a circle and
then up an inclined plane on the other side so that when a man goes
in it his head is at one moment hanging down like the flies on a
ceiling. Did you ever whirl round a hoop with a glass of water on
the rim?

[Mary also wrote to her mother from Blagdon:]

Today is very snowy and unpleasant, so that we have not stirred out
but have been sitting drawing at home and Charles has read to us
Macaulay's essay in the *Edinburgh*. He rode over to Morpeth to look
at the Rectory which is now nearly ready for the Greys.[1] He says it
is very nice.

Matt is extremely gracious and occupies himself a good deal with
his own affairs, and Cecilia looks quite charmingly and has twiddled
herself up very well. Mr. Saville Ogle[2] and Mr. Burrell[3] were here
last night. The latter is a clergyman with one arm, very pleasing
and gentlemanlike. The former rather a prig with some pretentions
to cleverness and very little foundation for it. The curate, Mr.
Bastard, seems a good sort of man—frank and honest and very
awkward looking. We went one day to Gosforth and saw Mr. Charles
Brandling,[4] who seems an *insouciant*, dull sort of person. Cecilia's
twiddling up of bedrooms is quite charming. I will just tell you what
we do all day.

[1] The Rev. Francis Grey, sixth son of the second Earl Grey of Howick,
was Rector of Morpeth for many years. He married, in 1840, Lady
Elizabeth Howard, daughter of the Earl of Carlisle and sister of Charles
Howard.

[2] Saville Ogle (1811–54) of Kirkley Hall, Northumberland. M.P. for
South Northumberland 1841–52. Married Mary Anne Wilson.

[3] The Rev. Matthew Burrell, second son of William Burrell of
Broome Park, was Vicar of Chatton 1844–69.

[4] Lt.-Col. Charles Brandling (1797–1856), only son of Ralph Brandling of Gosforth Park. He married in 1824 Henrietta, youngest
daughter of Sir George Armytage, Bart.

We generally walk out before luncheon, and work after luncheon down in the saloon, and after dinner sit and talk very quietly and soberly and Cecilia does the honours very well, and I make plenty of strong green tea to keep the people lively. I have been absorbed in *The Fair Maid of Perth* and have also been drawing a great deal. I wish I could draw all the things I imagine. I should like to be able to put down on paper all the things that strike me and that I fancy I could do until I begin to try and find it quite impossible—things out of Shakespeare, etc.

Cecilia's servants are all very nice—her maid quite a treasure and her Groom of the Chambers charming. She is quite comfortably established and as active and energetic as possible. Did I tell you of her touching appeal to the housekeeper's feelings when Lord Ossulston was coming? The woman seemed quite unwilling to air the bed. After exerting all her powers of persuasion Cecilia at last said: "You know Lord Ossulston is very delicate and if he dies it will be your fault." There was no resisting that, and Mrs. Slight was quite vanquished.

Thank dear Alice for her German epistle, and the shoes will do quite well to come when Aunt Fitzroy comes. I think I should like a few pairs of my silk stockings to come too then, as it is extravagant wearing the best new ones every evening. Also a certain white skirt with three tucks and work which is at present dirty and attached to a filthy waist —at least either that or the one over pink muslin to wear for common.

I am quite entirely fascinated by a pattern of chintz Francis Grey has got from Miles and Edwards—ivy on a white ground, perfectly lovely, 1s and 9d a yard. I wish you wanted some. I should like to twiddle some into the rooms at Blagdon. It would look so gay and pretty. I wish you would have some for something or other. I ordered a bag for the carriage. It will be a charming contrivance and do for shawls and habit etc.

Goodbye, it only wants a quarter of an hour to dinner,

Your loving child, Mary Howard.

[It was a very happy interlude for Cecilia. After they had gone she wrote to her mother:]

Charles and Mary are just gone in the midst of a perfect hurricane of wind. I am very unhappy at losing them. We have been so happy together and Charles is such a dear, good, charming brother. It is delightful to look forward to having them every year. Did you ever know that Charles might have had the living of Morpeth but objected to the creed of St. Athanasius and therefore would not go into the Church. When we were looking over the parsonage the other day he said he might have had it himself, and then how nice it would have been.[1] However, perhaps Mary's lot is one more suited to her, on the whole. She is as gay as a lark and it is quite funny sometimes to see Charles open his eyes wide with astonishment at some of her pranks. He seems so surprised, as if he had never seen the like before. Mary was not charmed with Mrs. Cookson at all. She did not come up to my description of her.

The Greys are here now—she writing a letter, he reading a novel. He is an odd mixture of levity and earnestness, going so far both ways. Almost a buffoon and devoted to dancing and novels and singing, and yet a great Puseyite, determined on having daily service, fasting and Saints' Days. The Morpeth folk were afraid he would be too severe, but his first act was ordering a modern novel, which dispelled their fears. He is bad tempered and a little sharp but when in a good humour very merry and good fun.

Heseltine is full of anxiety about my new room. Her whole mind is full of it and she is bent on twiddling up a *toilette* cover of new and elegant construction. I think it is very nice of her to be so interested. Do you not think I had better raise her wages to twenty guineas? She does so much and has been so good this year, both during my confinement and now acting as housekeeper as well.

November 1842   *Blagdon*

Dearest Papa, I have got a new pen on purpose to write to you, hearing that you accuse me of bad penmanship and feeling in my conscience that the accusation is not unfounded.

I went to see the inspection on the Town Moor, where there was a large assembly of ladies and a great crowd of the dirty inhabitants of

[1] The living was in the gift of his father, the Earl of Carlisle.

Newcastle all looking on with admiring eyes. The inspecting officer was Colonel Rotton, a huge jovial-looking moustachioed man in a splendid uniform and mounted on a fine prancing steed, altogether presenting a striking contrast to the tiny Colonel of the Yeomanry, who was perched on a shabby white poney and looked very insignificant. This splendid Hussar only arrived the night before from York, and having taken up his abode at the Turk's Head, sent a note to Mr. Bell at the mess to inform him that he had orders from the Horse Guards to inspect the troops and wished to know what arrangements were to be made. Mr. Bell thought it was a hoax and suspected certain individuals and therefore sent no answer, till presently came a message asking for one, and then he said "Oh tell him I'll send Jem Cookson with an answer presently." This went on for some time, but at last someone who was staying at the Turk's Head said there certainly was a large man with moustachios just arrived, and another said Colonel Rotton did answer that description, so poor Mr. Bell was all dismay and had to sit down and pen a humble apology. I do not think the horses were as good as those at York—some were so small and some such raw-boned creatures.

We have no water now, all the springs are dried up and there are carts perpetually bringing water all the day, which the oldest man cannot recollect happening before. I believe the new colliery [at Seaton Burn] has something to do with it. Baby has now been introduced to all the good folks who belong to Blagdon. The last was the ancient painter whom you may perhaps recollect taking care of the stove in church, clad in a scarlet comforter and brown scratch wig. He says he is the only man about here who can now say he has seen the fifth generation and expresses great admiration of Baby.

November 1842   *Blagdon*

Dearest Mama, Once again I am left a *widder*. Matt is gone away for one night to stand Godfather to Mrs. Bryan Burrell's baby.[1]

---

[1] Bryan Burrell (1805–81) was the eldest son of Mr. William Burrell of Broome Park. He married in 1837 Frances Mary, daughter of John Quantock of Somerset. They had three children, born in 1839, 1842 and 1843.

The dinner at Gosforth was rather amusing. The Charles Brand-lings were there and he is getting quite blue with taking nitrate of silver for fits. She is very dull. Miss Brandling[1] talks for all the family: she is dreadfully thin and Miss Fanny looks very silly,[2] so I am not fascinated with any of them. They presented me with a waltz composed by one of them and illustrated by another.

I must tell you that nasty old *Timothy Tiresome*[3] at Stannington has now requested to pull up all the evergreens near the church, pretending that the people object to them, and the real fact being that they are rather in the way of his *mowing*. He has mown away the only *cedar* we had, which we had put there in a good place. He went with me last year to choose the place for planting them and he never minded a bit how much the people objected to his horses then— tiresome old man. We will not take the plants away.

[On 13 November 1842 Lady Parke's mother, Mrs. Barlow, died. Cecilia wrote to her mother:]

Blagdon

I have just received your letter. I am sure you must be upset, notwithstanding the reasons we have had for expecting the event. Poor dear Grandmama, I am sure for her sake no one can grieve at the change which must be, to her, so blessed. Yet we here must mourn for the loss of such a dear, virtuous old lady. May we, her grandchildren, be as worthy of her as you, dearest Mama. I cannot bear to bother you about my things. I do not understand from your letter whether one of the four black bonnets is for me or no. If it is I shall be very glad of it, and also of the bugle flowers and bertha and rosettes. If you really think my figured silk would do, I think my best plan will be to have a black velvet made with a morning and evening waist, which will be sufficient for me, and I should like to have a good deal

[1] Miss Emma Brandling, sister of Charles Brandling of Gosforth Park.
[2] Miss Fanny Brandling, first cousin of Emma and Charles, daughter of Robert Brandling of Low Gosforth. She married, as his second wife, Col. Harry Armytage, brother of Mrs. Charles Brandling.
[3] The Rev. Timothy Myers, Vicar of Stannington.

of black crape sent, as it so soon gets shabby—perhaps thirteen yards.
I should like to have the open sleeves, so will you be so good as to send
me what is wanted for them and also a few collars, as I could not get
them nice here. I think goffering irons would be very useful to me.
If you did not intend the bonnet for me, never mind. Do not let the
other things wait, for I could not make my velvet do. I have been
consulting Heseltine and she says it would not do to have the striped
silk with bands of crape, and there is not enough to make any of the
same, so in that case I must have a good plain silk, sixteen yards, and
make up the striped one for an evening. I have in London an old
white satin gown. I think I shall write to Malloch to have it dyed
and you could perhaps send me a black lace or net dress to put over,
if you think that would do for me. Do you think I should want velvet
too? And what can I do for *every* evening? I am ashamed for all this
bother for you. Heseltine's idea is that the striped silk is not deep
enough to be trimmed with crape. I have a black watered silk for
common. Goodbye, dearest Mama, your affectionate child, C. R.

[Lady Parke lost no time in sending the mourning which seems to
have concerned Cecilia more than any other aspect of her grandmother's death, for only five days later she wrote to Alice:]

November 1842   *Blagdon*

All the things Mama sent came quite well and as I took them out
I felt quite astonished at the trouble Mama had taken for me and the
forethought in every little thing, and at such a time too, when her
thoughts must have been engrossed so sorrowfully. It will be a trying
journey for her: I hope her health may not suffer . . . I have often
and often fancied I could almost see our dear little brother as a little
angel watching us from Heaven, and now that dear Grandmama is
there I feel as if she were another tie to bind us there.

. . . What will poor Aunt Fanny do?

[Lady Parke had evidently complained of Cecilia's habit of never
dating any of her letters, for in the next one she more than adequately
did so. Alas, however, she did not maintain the custom and it is the

only one of all her letters that she dated. But Lady Parke and the Baron were offenders in the same way. It is odd, in view of the fact that they all preserved each other's letters, that they none of them bothered to date any.]

Sunday evening, 4 December 1842   *Library, Blagdon*
Dearest Mama, Did you not think of the beam and the mote when you begged me to date my letters? Thanks many for the bugle beauties. They are quite pets and I wish you would send Mary some as a gift from me—she would like them I think. I cannot make up my mind to incur the responsibility of glove tops at present.

Our party went off all right I think. Everybody was lively and pleasant and there was much talk and fun. On Tuesday we go to Meldon, to the old Cooksons, for two days and I hope we shall go somewhere else soon. I like now and then going away for a day or two, and I think it does one good. Baby is not quite well. I consulted Sir John Fife, who gave him grey powder, which I told you I believe, and who afterwards advised giving up the asses' milk, for every time he took it he was much worse. Wells has been in excellent humour for a fortnight, but today she is tiresome again, so grumbling and she seems not to speak out and to be always *fancying* that I *fancy* things. She thinks the house is shocking, she says: she believes everyone must be ill in it: it is so close and damp. Now I do not at all agree with her, for although the soil is damp the house inside is as dry as possible. And if it were not, what is the use of bothering and tormenting me about that, for I cannot build a new house. This is my home where I and Baby must pass our lives. I think, however, I shall change the nursery and put him upstairs, for that room in which he is now is rather small and close and too hemmed in by trees, and now that I do not nurse there is no objection to his being upstairs. I do not expect that she will be satisfied with the room there, for even in London she found great fault with that charming large room she used to have. I wish I had courage to give her a good rattle, but if I did I think she would not bear it. Our gardener has given notice and intends to go, which is a good thing. We mean to write to Edinburgh for a successor. There is a famous nursery garden there where people get

excellent gardeners. I will ask the Knight of the Souffles all you wish
to know tomorrow. Mrs. Wallace's star is still in the ascendant.

Goodbye, dearest Mother. Best love to Papa.

Your loving daughter
Cecilia Ridley.

Sunday evening, Dec. 4th 1842, Library, Blagdon.
Sunday evening, Dec. 4th 1842.
Sunday evening, Dec. 4th 1842.
Sunday evening, Dec. 4th 1842.

6 December 1842   *Meldon, Morpeth*

Dearest Alice, Behold me after a long, coldish, dampish drive arrived
at Meldon, turned into a large bedroom smelling strongly of the
upholsterer, with nearly an hour to spare before dinner. What shall
I do? I think I will write to my sister Alice, that little busy maiden
seeking for great men, cantering to court and balancing a bubble.
You really seem well occupied now and I think it must be very
interesting. If I discover a new great man I will let you know, but I
am not exactly in the way of so doing. However do pray read the
review of Milton in an old *Edinburgh* by Macaulay, quite splendid.[1]

I have been busy changing Baby's nursery. He is going into Matt's
old room upstairs, and another large room to sleep in, so he will be
very grand. He is such a pet, you would be quite pleased with him
I am sure. I have put my bird into his room and it is not thrown
away upon him. He sits crowing to it and watching it constantly, and
he has also got an India rubber rattle and a small fat tumbler. I have
found a large beautiful toyshop at Newcastle and if you like I will
send you a doll from it. Our camellias are beautiful now and we have
much better flowers than we had last year. My table covers get on
rather slowly but they *do* get on and both will look well I think. One
will be very large all in crochet and coarse wool of bright colours, which
is very amusing work.

I bore the news of Lady Ridley's ill looks with great fortitude.

[1] It had appeared in the *Edinburgh Review* for August 1825.

excellent gardeners. I
will not the Knight
of the Souffles tell you
wish to know tomorrow.
Mrs Wallace's store is
still in the ascendent

Goodbye dearest Mother
Best love to Papa
Your loving daughter
Cecilia Reilly

Sunday eve. Dec. 4th 1842
Library Blagdon

Sunday eve. Dec 4th 1842
Sunday eve. Dec 4th 1842
Sunday eve Dec 4th 1842

8 December 1842   *Blagdon*

Dearest Mama, The enclosed waited at Meldon, for the ridiculous butler could not give or sell or lend any stamps and I had none and could not make up my mind to steal. As for the Moncks, I do not think we shall go on there, for Lady Mary wrote me a note saying that now as we were quite established on our respective visiting lists we need not take the trouble to call any more, and that she hoped the time *might come* when we could go and stay at each other's houses.

The ball is next Thursday and I think I might either wear a white camellia or a twist of silver and velvet if it is not too soon, so I think I will not go to the expense of a *cordon*.

I have been distributing prizes at the schools. I sent to the Christian Knowledge Society for part of them and they were more than two months in getting them, so they did not arrive till last week. The Plessey master wished to have a prize for each child to avoid making any jealousies, but I thought fourteen out of forty children would be quite enough and yesterday I sallied forth to give them. He was very much obliged and he made all the children stand in a row before me and at the same moment make a bow or a curtsey and say Thank you. It almost made me laugh but I kept my countenance. I am afraid we shall not be able to get a good master from the National Society for Stannington. However I have written a full description of the school to Mr. Jennings and I thought it as well to say that Stannington was a bleak dirty place, for I fear a south country man would not like it. I have been busy arranging my shells and Mr. Adamson is going to help me. There are a few in Park Street that I mean to purloin and if you care for it I can take several up to replace them with. My collection here will be very nice I expect. I think it will be a nice amusement to Baby when he is bigger. He is extremely noisy and rather mischievous and shows a beginning of character, so that I feel all the anxiety and responsibility of education beginning. He is very good, and I am sure he has a charming temper. I think Wells manages him very well. She is more noisy with him than Madame Necker[1] approves, and possibly she may be inclined to make him rather of too

[1] Albertine A. Necker, author of *L'Éducation Progressive* (Brussels 1840).

C.R.—H

much consequence and importance, more than would be good for him when he is older, but that is easily prevented and will go off a good deal when there is another. She took upon herself to order anything she liked for him herself without asking me, which I was obliged to put a stop to.

CHAPTER TEN

Spring 1843

CECILIA was by this time expecting another baby. They remained at Blagdon for the rest of the hunting season, and the letters continue to record the daily incidents of her life at home and among the neighbours:

The chief events of the county are the adventures of poachers and keepers who are constantly having battles either in one place or another. The last remarkable one was at old Mr. Ogle's,[1] where a poacher was shot by his companion and killed on the spot, being mistaken for a keeper. The huntsman's account of it was: "A pawcher shot a pawcher and I was voy glad it torned oot that way." We are saved much annoyance by not watching, and I really think I should not like to risk people's lives in doing so. However, old Cuddie has warlike propensities and would be ready at any time to fight pawchers if allowed.

We are going to have all the Bells here next week and various other people besides. Perhaps I shall learn to like them, but I do not think I shall or can ever have any affection for a creature with the name of Bell. There is a sort of *country townishness* about all those I have ever seen which is very remarkable I think.

I am busy reading James's *Louis XIV*[2] and am much interested, though I should like to beat the man for his ridiculous style. I wish Macaulay would write a history—how clear and impressive it would be. I am also studying gardening books and mean to become very

---

[1] John Ogle (1767–1853) of Kirkley Hall.
[2] *The Life and Times of Louis XIV* by G. P. R. James (1838).

distinguished in that line like Mrs. Cadogan,[1] who, according to her husband's account, did not know a rose from a cabbage a year ago and now manages gardens and greenhouses entirely herself and expresses the greatest astonishment that anyone can live without gardening. She is so funny—she has her horses clipped and singed in her own way and superintends the stable management as you do the kitchen. She is too horse-and-doggy for me, and I like her husband much the best of the two.

January 1843   *Blagdon*

Yesterday I had a long visit from Lady Elizabeth Grey and she did me a great deal of good by her nice kind conversation. She is going to get Mr. Fenwick[2] to meet me to luncheon and I shall talk about schools. William Ridley and Major Tempest[3] came here yesterday and I think it has done me good to have them. At any rate I am really much better and more *up* today. I cannot say much for our conversation however, for Major Tempest splutters on and packs his words up so closely that one cannot distinguish them. But he makes talk and is good natured and William is very kind and quiet. He is very fat and eating much but a very good tempered, kind hearted creature.

Lady Ridley sent me a little bag which she had knitted, so tidily and ingeniously made that she must have found employment for months in it. I shall try and copy it.

We had the huge curate at dinner yesterday, telling of all his exploits in keeping the farmers in order. He threatens them with all kinds of dreadful things, which he says he has lawful power to do to

[1] Sarah Cadogan, only daughter of Ward Cadogan of Brinkburn Priory, Northumberland, married Major William Hodgson, who assumed by Royal Licence, on the death of his father-in-law in 1835, the additional surname and arms of Cadogan.

[2] John Fenwick (1787–1867), attorney and antiquary of Newcastle. He was a "staunch and argumentative Baptist", but he co-operated with members of other denominations to promote schemes of "piety and benevolence". He was one of the founders of the Newcastle Law Society.

[3] Thomas Richard Tempest of Tong Hall, Yorks., was a Major in the 6th or Duke of York's Own Rifle Corps.

make them do as he wants them, so that I should think they must have a perfect horror of him. He gets into shocking scrapes—he is so violent and inconsiderate. Amongst other things the Bishop of Durham has been very anxious to put a stop to the practice, so common here, of people going off to Newcastle to be married, and has desired it to be remedied. Mr. Bastard, hearing that a man was going to be married at Newcastle, went off, looked into all the register books in all the parishes and at last found it entered and the banns three times published. Upon which he wrote in the book "Stopt Stannington Parish" but never told the man, who, the next day, went all the way there with his bride and friends and was disappointed. I do not think Mr. Myers will last long. I wonder who will have the living then. It is in the Bishop's gift, but I do not know whether he is always particular in his choice. We want a very sensible, discreet good man very much, and an active one too.

Will you tell me in your next how long I ought to wear mourning? And if I have my other black silk made, how the sleeves should be? I am still just the same, taking stout and getting into cold water every morning. Perhaps I am a little nearer being quite well—I think I am.

[The next letter was written from Benwell, now a part of Newcastle, where her sister-in-law Sarah Cookson lived:]

I must write you a little note today. We came here on Tuesday and it has not been at all disagreeable, except that last night I had such a dreadful sick headache that I was obliged to leave the dinner table and go to bed. I think it was caused by Mr. Dawson's tonic which was too strong. . . . The children here are so plain I cannot take to them, and they will insist upon calling the plainest the image of my little Matt, which is not true, for mine looks quite like a gentleman, though he is not handsome, and the other is a thorough Cookson. I liked my visit to Fenham, though I cannot endure the manners of the fair Milly Bell.[1] She exhibited the fishing and shooting

[1] "Fair Milly" was the youngest child of Robert Bell (see page 74). She was born in 1816 and married Matthew Bigge.

dresses she had worn in Scotland and also the gown she is to have as bridesmaid to Janetta Ridley. She was in great *embarras* concerning the shawl or scarf to wear with the latter, so I offered her my black lace cardinal and thought myself very good natured. However, she found something else that would do better.

Mrs. Headlam dined there one day and entertained me with long histories of her excessive intimacy with Lady Ridley—how she used to try on her gowns and even her *drawers*, and how they used to cook beef steaks together. One cannot fancy the great lady condescending to such frolics. I believe it was partly a ruse of the old Mrs. Headlam to make me have her to stay with me more, but I do not like her at all, at all.

We go to Ravensworth next week. We were to have gone also to Beaufront[1] where dwelleth Mrs. Cuthbert, *née* Cookson, but her brother in law, Mr. Shadwell, having died, our visit is postponed.

February 1843   *Blagdon*

Baby has been troubled with his teeth, so I sent for Sir John Fife who lanced his gums yesterday and he is more comfortable. The moment Sir John came into the room he said "I see what we must do, we must bind your ears down, they stick off so." And he then recommended me to make him wear thin linen nightcaps, as otherwise, he says, the ears will stick off more and more and increase in size and look very ugly. Wells was quite offended and rather grumpy all day and thought it great nonsense, but I shall get him the caps, I think, for really it will be tiresome if he grows up with large, sticking-off ears.

Janetta Ridley was married this week and there was a great gathering from all parts for the occasion. Sir Charles Monck filled Belsay to overflowing and the marriage took place from there. I really think it was a very kind thing to do and not many people would have taken so much trouble. The bride and bridegroom are gone abroad for four months and are then to settle down for

---

[1] Beaufront Castle, Corbridge-on-Tyne, designed by Dobson in 1837 to look like a castle from the railway line, is still lived in by the Cuthberts.

life near Newcastle. They will probably have nearly a thousand a year.

[As Janetta was the cause of the family quarrel it is not surprising that she was not married from Blagdon, but strange that Cecilia did not even attend the wedding. Janetta had made her home with her elder sister, Laura Monck, but she never lived near Newcastle after her marriage, as she and Isaac Cookson spent their married life in the Argentine, where Janetta died in 1867 of yellow fever, and her husband shortly after of "softening of the brain."]

February 1843   *Blagdon*

There came a letter yesterday from the dame of Seymour Place[1] which Matt read to me, in which *à propos* to nothing at all was a very decided opinion against ladies having anything to do with *schools* and teaching, saying they had done immense mischief and bringing as an instance a Miss Shuttleworth, a great heiress, who had taken to building schools and ended by marrying a violent dissenting minister at Hastings.[2] Likewise it contained a hit at the Ravensworths, saying how times were changed with Lady R., who had once spoken so warmly against ladies acting and had interfered, Lady Ridley thought very improperly, to prevent Lady Normanby acting at Florence. All this is spite and nothing else.

I have been deep in *Ten Thousand a Year*[3] and seldom have thought a book more interesting, although it certainly is long and the details sometimes tedious. Mr. Subtle paring his nails delighted me but I should have been very glad to have had Papa now and then to tell me who the people were. I do not know Mr. Lynx unless it be

[1] Lady Ridley was now living in Seymour Place in London.

[2] Janet Shuttleworth of Gawthorpe near Burnley. She married Dr. James Kay, a Nonconformist but not a minister, and an eminent educational pioneer.

[3] A very popular novel by Samuel Warren published in 1839. Warren was a barrister and M.P. for Midhurst. He was the author of many legal textbooks and also of *Passages from the Diary of a Late Physician.*

Milord Campbell. The Marquis Gants Jaunes de Mille Fleurs I suppose is Count D'Orsay, of course. I strongly advise you to read it by all means. Do ask Papa who Mr. Crafty is?

February or March 1843   *Blagdon*

I liked my visit at Ravensworth extremely. Lady Ravensworth was most kind and we had lovely walks, for the weather was exactly like summer. They were all so kind and charming and there was no one there except Mr. Blakeney[1] and a middle aged neighbour with spreading whiskers. I saw the place to great advantage and admired it far more than I had imagined before. The walks about it are, I think, charming, and there are two broad grass terraces at the west end of the Castle which are perfectly delightful.

Great events are going on here. There is really going to be a girls' school, and I have settled the plan of my flower garden. I am wicked enough to feel rather sorry that the said school is not my own doing and that it would have been built and arranged now even if I had not been here. But that is very selfish and I am really delighted to get the school anyhow. The parish is in a great state of excitement owing to late disturbances,—and I have followed your example and given much advice to Mr. Bastard respecting his goings on. He says he is extremely obliged to me and will now try gentle means instead of violent ones.

I wish I could say exactly when we are to go to town. We talk of it and always end by settling nothing, for there is this tiresome hunting going on and I know Matt will take several days to make all his arrangements before leaving home. However, I hope we shall be fairly started by the end of Easter week and I am very anxious to go soon, for I think I must be at home again in July.

19 April 1843   *Blagdon*

Indeed it is a great delight to think of seeing you so soon after such a long, long separation. I am looking forward to showing Baby

[1] Mr. Blakeney was tutor to the large Liddell family. He lived "all the winters of his life" at Ravensworth and was adored by all the family to whom he left his money when he died.

to you with the greatest delight. He is really a darling and I think everyone must think him so. Yesterday I took him to see Mrs. Loraine who has a baby the same age and twice as fat—a perfect mountain that gave one quite the feeling of a Brobdingnag child. It had thick eyebrows and dark hair and looked like a fat old man dressed as a baby. Little Matt was quite amazed and could not bear his large contemporary.

I cannot say quite what day we shall be in London, as we have had no answer from the Richard Ridleys. The chariot is all ready and waiting for me. I cannot help suspecting that little Miss Howard will arrive before partridge shooting, and I feel certain my little daughter will.

CHAPTER ELEVEN

Little Eddy

THERE are no letters for the summer of 1843, when Cecilia was in London and seeing her mother every day. She returned to Blagdon at the end of July to await the birth of her next baby. On her arrival she wrote:

I am delighted to be here in summer and quite charmed to see all my roses out and to eat my own strawberries. Have you any blue gentian? It is the best of the blues and beautiful just now, and we have a pretty Banksia rose in flower against the wall, in little yellow clusters. The greenhouse now looks very gay and we have a great variety of pretty things . . . I think I shall have nothing but verbenas and nemophilas in the little garden I made this year, which is this way—the middle raised in three stages and sixteen little beds round it.

I have got a schoolmistress who is very promising and the school is at last begun, which is a satisfaction. I find everything going on as usual, Mr. Bastard not improved in discretion: he tells me that two or three women never came to church all the time I was away and make a point of being very regular when I am here, but that I shall take no notice of.

August 1843   *Blagdon*

Alas, it rains and all my plans of sitting out of doors and sketching from a haycock are put an end to. We are all very well and the poor nurserymaid going on favourably. The surgeon has not been able yet to set the arm but says he can do so tomorrow. There is not a chance of her being able to use it for two months, so I am going to try and get one of my former ones for the time. Really I cannot bear the very word nurserymaid and I wonder Mr. Denison did not discover something concerning them in my horoscope. I am sorry to say Wells has got the black day and I have secretly determined that I will not keep her when I go next year to town unless she is quite altered. Baby is extremely well and gay and I fancy he recognises his old nursery. I am quite settled now and very comfortable and find myself much stronger and able to walk about beautifully. I thought myself looking remarkably well, too, and was altogether in spirits about it when, to my disappointment, Mr. Park the groom told me that he did not consider that I looked at all well. There has been a great cleaning going on during our absence—papering, painting, colouring etc. and two new beds which look very nice and fresh and the chintzes very pretty.

August 1843   *Blagdon*

The rain it raineth every day. Alas when will it cease? I am weary of it and I believe the bailiff will go out of his mind if it continues, as the hay will be spoilt. Today Matt goes out to meet the judges with the High Sheriff, and tomorrow he will be on the Grand Jury, but he will get off the dinners in the evening I think, for I should not like to be left alone tomorrow or Friday night. The High Sheriff is in the same predicament as to *his* wife and intends riding home twenty miles every night, which will be hard work. . . . Goodbye, dearest Mama, I am extremely well and quite ready now for coming events: indeed I hope I shall not wait long, for my evening gown will not last beyond a few days.

On 12 August at 56 Park Street Mary Howard gave birth to a son, George, who ultimately became the ninth Earl of Carlisle. Cecilia wrote to her mother the next day:

I am quite enchanted with the news. It is really delightful to have got it over so happily and to have a nice little son. Dear, sweet Mary, how I should like to see her with her baby. I can hardly believe she can be a Mama, it seems so very strange. You see, after all, you were right when you said she would be first. How very fortunate that you were not gone to Ampthill, for if she had been left alone and unprepared it would have been a dreadful affair. The little son will be obliged to turn out a sportsman, being born on the 12th of August. I long to know what he is like—whether he is large or small and whether he is very red. In short all particulars concerning his appearance and manners and whether he has much hair in particular. The moment I read your letter I rushed upstairs and announced the news to both Heseltine and Wells who were much pleased, and Wells, when I told her Mary had been out to dine the same day, said she wished I would go out more to bring it on, and that I should move about more. She does not know by experience that one cannot skip about as if nothing was going on, and I am always out walking until I am quite amazed at myself.

16 August *Blagdon*

I trust dearest Mary has got through her third day happily and is establishing herself as a nurse without annoyance or pain. I wonder if her baby is like mine at all? How does she manage without a room through hers, and has she a *sucking pot* like that most delightful one of mine?

We are all very well and I am particularly so, though quite enormous and rather fearful that there must be two chicks to cause such size. I am quite ashamed of having had Mrs. Ramsay so long . . . I did not go to church today, being advised not. We are meditating the purchase of a donkey for Baby, as he is so heavy and when there is another baby to carry too it will be hard work.

[How well one knows those days of waiting for an overdue baby, and the feeling of guilt at keeping the monthly nurse waiting. A sucking pot is what we should call a feeding cup—a cup with a spout.

On 19 August Lady Parke replied to this letter:]

I hardly know how to greet your handwriting with pleasure, though I daresay you have been wrong in your calculations and that the young lady is only taking her just and lawful time, and she will come into the world with all the strength and perfection that belongs to her. Darling Mary certainly feels the weather, it is so dreadfully hot. She makes a good nurse, but I think she may find it rather a drag upon her, though we shall better judge of this by and bye. She uses a sucking pot, but the Old Crab thinks that she sucks in wind and she will not allow us to feed Mary, as she says that moving her arm to cut her meat is good to circulate the milk. Mary has had chicken and mutton chop and simple jelly merely made with calves foot leaves, sugar and sherry and a few caraway seeds in it, merely a very small *pinch*. She is to have her first glass of porter today, which I almost dread, poor child, fearing it may make her head ache.

I am rejoiced to hear that the small Matt is so well and so browned with the sun. I have really no patience with Wells—I daresay her temper is beyond control. What an evil it is to herself to be so subject to these fits of crossness. I really think nurses are great torments.

[The next day, 20 August, Cecilia's baby was born. It was not the young lady that Lady Parke anticipated, but another boy, who was called Edward, after Lady Ridley's half-brother, Sir Edward Bowater. The night he was born Heseltine wrote to Lady Parke:]

My Lady, Sir Matthew will of course write by the post, but I, knowing your anxiety, write to say her Ladyship had an excellent time. We sent for the doctor a quarter before five, and a quarter past six he was in the house and just in time, for Lady R. was taken at five, indeed she was out at four and said before going we were not to go far, as she was not very well. At half past six a fine boy was born but I never saw anything so quick. A few minutes after he was born Lady R. said it is nothing to the last, I don't care *to have one every week*. She has had tea and toast and gruel and biscuits since and is really quite charming. Sir Matthew would not believe it was over when word was sent. The baby has dark hair and is in every respect at present like her Ladyship, having a nice forehead and eyes, and sucked his thumb half an hour after he was born. I have just seen him take a spoonful of castor oil and quietly go to sleep.

I went to Lady R. but she been asleep. I did not say I was writing to you or am sure I should have had a long message. I hope Mrs. Howard is well. I have heard she is a good nurse, having plenty of milk. At present Lady R. has very little. Baby was tried but would not suck. I will write your Ladyship tomorrow. I remain your most obedient servant, C. Heseltine.

Master Ridley is quite well but does not much like the baby, as he appears sensible there is another to love.

[Meanwhile Mary was not at all well. Her mother became anxious about her two days before Cecilia's baby was born, but she did not develop any serious symptoms until 20 August, and she died on the 26th, as the result, obviously, of an infective illness, but whether it was puerperal sepsis or pneumonia is difficult to say. There is a tradition in the Howard family that it was attributable to faulty drains at Park Street. Cecilia was not told the tragic news for a week, for fear of upsetting her too much so soon after her own confinement, and then she was told by Sir Matthew, followed up by this letter from her father:]

7 September 1843   *Ampthill*

My beloved Cecilia, Before this meets your eye, you will have been told that sad truth, which the tender care and prudence of your dear husband has long concealed from you, that you have lost your darling sister and that the strong tie of affection which has united you ever since you had each the power of reason, and existed without the interruption of a single minute, has been broken by the hand of Death. It has pleased God, in His inscrutable wisdom, to take away from her afflicted parents, sisters and friends, that dear creature, the delight of our home, and the charm of our society, so beautiful and so gay, and as good as she was gay. But we must learn to bear this great affliction, and God, I hope, will give me strength to support it, and grace to profit by it, so that through the means of a wise holy life I may be rendered fit to meet the blessed spirit of my sweet angel again.

Your mother will probably have given you an account of the early period of our sweet Mary's illness. As soon as she had been safely delivered I went to Ampthill, every appearance being favourable. This was on the 12th of August. On Wednesday the 16th I was sent for to Croydon, and on passing through town saw my dear child, to all appearance well. She continued so till Friday the 18th, when your dear mother was a little uncomfortable about her, but no more, for Dr. Farr, who attended her, assured your mother that there was not even a drawback. On Saturday she sat up; on Sunday and Monday she was weak, apparently from the great heat of the weather. On Tuesday Dr. Ferguson was sent for, who thought she was going to be ill, and on Wednesday it appeared clear that she had an attack of fever, which, after a long resistance, ultimately overcame her. Between Wednesday and Friday morning we had all the vicissitudes of hope, sometimes strong and sometimes weak, but very early on the latter morning, Charles, that dear, good, virtuous and amiable man who, during almost the whole of her illness, was sitting quiet at the bedside of his beloved wife, came to tell us that her pulse, which usually abated in the morning, had not done so, and we then gave ourselves up to despair. I had told Dr. Farr that I wished to see her before she was no more, and at half past ten on Friday morning he sent to me to come up immediately, as life was ebbing fast away. My beloved child greeted me with a look of the warmest affection, and pressed my hand in a manner which showed her filial love. Her bedside was crowded round by your dear mother, Charles, Lady Caroline Lascelles (as good a creature as her brother) and Mrs. Fitzroy. On all she cast looks of ineffable sweetness, assured us she was better, "quite well," and did everything to make us suppose she underwent no suffering. To a question of Dr. Farr's whether she knew where she was going, she intimated that she did and assured us she was happy, and who could doubt it from her countenance, which looked angelical—beaming with intelligence and the most touching affection and calmness? Oh! she was too beautiful. After this, life was supported by stimulants and restoratives for about sixteen hours, during which time she was asleep for four, her pulse then became steady, and we were indulging the vain hope that even then life might be supported until the fever abated. But this did not last long. She awoke and complained of a great pain in her side, which she attributed to a blister, that Dr. Latham, who attended her, thought it necessary to put on. Charles was bursting into tears at her side, with her hands clasped in his. She smiled on him and said "Oh! it did me no harm," anxious to soothe his pain.

She was sensible to the last, and whenever her weakness permitted her to speak, she gave some expression of her happy feeling; and when she was silent her looks assured us of it. About midnight on Friday the stimulants began to lose their effect. I held her wrist and the pulse became faint, and life was on the wing. At that moment she held up both her arms in the attempt to embrace her beloved husband, with a look of the tenderest love, and soon after fell back and expired. She was endeavouring to utter many words but in vain. I listened with my ear close, and thought (but I cannot say more than that) it was possible she said "Sisters, sisters, sisters," those being the only very dear friends she did not see at her bedside. She had talked about you and her child the day before, the last of her life.

My dear child, you know, perhaps better than I do, what a treasure we have lost, for you lived with her every hour of the day, knew what intelligence, what temper, what cheerfulness, what an appetite for knowledge, what love of the good and beautiful, what deep-seated piety, what happy religious feelings she had. Since her departure to another and far happier existence (happy as hers always was here, for her life was one of perpetual sunshine) we have looked amongst her books and found in what channels her thoughts ran in the calm of solitude . . .

I could fill sheets with these melancholy but not unpleasing topics, but for the present I have done. Hereafter we may discourse upon them, hardly without shedding tears but with calmness and comfort. Thank God! He has left me you, my beloved child, to comfort my old age, with your presence often, and always with delightful thoughts of virtue, intelligence and sweetness, such as our departed Mary has left with me for ever. He has left me also Alice, who bids fair to equal you both in everything which renders a woman such a blessing to the human race. I wish you all happiness, my beloved, to yourself, your husband and children, and I am

Ever your most affectionate Father,

J. Parke.

[Cecilia replied:]

11 September 1843   *Blagdon*

My dearest Papa, You know from my dear husband that he has at last told me of the great calamity with which it has pleased God to afflict us. He did all that was possible to prepare my mind for the sad truth, but such an event was so far from my thoughts that the blow could not fail to be stunning, and it was long before I could bring myself to believe that my bright, beautiful sister, whom I so dearly, so tenderly loved, was indeed taken from us. May God enable me to bear this deep affliction with calmness and resignation and to profit by it according to His will. On Saturday I had your letter, which has been to me a great comfort. I have read it over and over again and dwelt with melancholy pleasure on all the particulars of the happy and beautiful death of my sweet sister. ·God had indeed bestowed upon us a treasure in giving her to us, and most thankful ought we to feel that we have possessed His precious gift until now. From her childhood she has gladdened all around her with her sunny smile and her gay heart, and Oh! what a privilege, what a blessing, it was to me to have such a sister, to live so long with that sweet creature, and to know so well all the virtues and all the beauties of her charming character. Everything that I possess is full of recollections of her, and how I shall now treasure them up in my heart. She was to me a friend such as few are blessed with. Every thought, every feeling was known to her; every pursuit was in common with her and in everything she was to me as my guardian angel. *May* I not still look to her as such?

It has been a great comfort to me to hear daily good accounts of your health and to find that you have all been so mercifully supported. Dear Charles seems to be an example of true Christian resignation, and his loss is even greater than mine. Will you give him my love? I will write to my dearest mother tomorrow. She

C.R.—I

will be glad to hear, as you will also, how well I am and how thriving my darling baby continues. We think him like you and I trust he will grow up so. He is certainly very good tempered and has bright dark eyes and dark hair. Farewell for the present, my beloved Father.

[On 12 September Charles wrote himself:]

Ampthill

My dear Cecilia, I must beg your acceptance of the accompanying locket with dearest Mary's hair. It is very simple and has the merit of showing what it contains. I will not write to you more at present, but at some future time it will be a great consolation to talk with you about her and to dwell upon her bright and happy memory.

This place is most soothing. It is so full of her and we do each other good by talking about her. We are all wonderfully well. It is such a comfort having that conviction of her blessedness now and forever. We have been very grateful that you have submitted with resignation to this heavy blow. Sir Matthew has been very kind in sending to us daily accounts of your well doing and that of your baby.

Again I must wish you goodbye. God bless you,

Believe me, your affectionate,

Charles Howard.

CHAPTER TWELVE

Autumn 1843

CHARLES never married again. The baby was brought up by Lady Parke and "she goes about it as if it were her own youngest child," the Baron reported to Cecilia. For the rest of Cecilia's short life both she and her parents referred to Mary in almost every one of their letters to each other. I have left out most of these references, as they only repeat an inconsolable sense of loss combined with the firm conviction of Mary's happier and more blessed state. The physical cause of the death of this young and healthy girl was accepted with a complacency that is incredible to our generation. Although Cecilia gradually resumed an interest in her daily life, helped by her absorption in her children, she never wholly recovered her gaiety and lightness of heart.

20 September 1843   *Blagdon*

My baby continues to thrive. Tomorrow the nurse is to go and he will change his abode and go upstairs, which I feel quite sorry for. I like so much having him close to me all day and being able to watch him asleep. However, I trust I shall soon be strong enough to go constantly upstairs, for I feel every day more equal to exertion. The porter seems to suit me very well. I hope soon to be able to go about and see the poor people around me, but I am not quite strong enough yet. I drive out every day now, and yesterday I went through the village and saw the school, the outside of which is finished and looks neat. I expect much pleasure and interest from it.

We have written for rooms in a very nice clean hotel at Tynemouth. If we cannot get them we shall try to find a lodging, but they are said not to be so nice. Tomorrow I shall have been married two years —what things have happened in that time.

29 September 1843   *Tynemouth*

The weather here is cold but today it was much improved, so that I was able to sit on the Castle Hill all the afternoon and look at the beautiful sea with all the ships crossing the bar and entering the river. It is a very nice place—fine rocks and a beautiful old Abbey and a great deal of shipping, and the inn is very comfortable. The babies go out as much as possible and are washed in sea water every day. The little one is not perfectly well but nothing much the matter, only a slight derangement which I think may be my fault. Little Matt is the picture of health and delights in standing on the shore and filling his hands with sand. . . . Mary's best present to me just before I left London was that charming book on Education by Madame Necker which she liked so much.[1] I study it constantly and try to profit by it. It makes one feel very strongly what a great charge it is to be a mother. May I be but half as good a one as you, and my children will have cause to rejoice.

October 1843   *Tynemouth*

I do not think my *little* baby has at all increased in size during the last fortnight. He was not a large child, indeed I thought him small, but the nurse and doctor assured me he was quite the usual size, and during the month he certainly improved much. He looks healthy and his limbs are strong. He is washed in cold water, Wells being a great advocate of it (not at night). It did very well for little Matt. The doctor desired he should be washed in salt water here. We mean to stay till next Saturday if it continues fine.

11 October 1843   *Blagdon*

I am not comfortable about Baby, for he is not well. Not quite so bad as little Matt was last year but in the same way. Mr. Dawson was here this morning and comes tomorrow, and I think he will most likely recommend a wet nurse, but he seems rather anxious not to have one unless necessary. The poor little thing looks so pale and small with his large dark eyes and long eyelashes and he is so constantly crying it makes one wretched to hear him; and when he has

[1] See note, page 113.

intervals without pain and feels comfortable he begins to coo and smile so sweetly. I am afraid my nursing has been the cause at first of this, but he went on beautifully for the first month. I do so long to see you all and talk to you. I wish the journey was not so long, for I shall almost dread it for you in the winter. But still I hope you will come. I hardly hope to go to Ampthill now, and indeed I should not feel happy to leave Baby until he was quite well, which I fear may be some time.

The school at Stannington will soon be ready and I must try and make some arrangements about it, though I cannot do exactly as I like, it not being my own school. I daresay it will do well, and the prospect of it seems to give great satisfaction to the farmers etc. around. It will be a great pleasure if the girls become clean and respectable and make good useful servants afterwards.

[A very different idea of the purpose of education from what is held today, nor did Cecilia and her generation realise that the education of girls would lead to the disappearance of servants altogether. The school was started by the agent of Lord Carlisle, who owned the village of Stannington, and it is said by old people in the village, whose mothers attended it, that it was begun in order to protect the girls from the cruelty of Mr. Carrick, the schoolmaster who was in charge of the boys, and who used to beat the cripples with their own crutches. Two months later Cecilia reported:]

Yesterday the schoolmistress came to see her future home, and having lionised her I brought her home and had a long talk with her. Matt thinks the only fault he can find is that she does not look homely enough. However, she seems very satisfied and humble and I like her manner and her plans. Her house is very damp and wretched and the approach to it in such a state that one can hardly get to it, but she keeps saying she thinks it will be very comfortable. There are only two scholars but several more are expected, but Mr. Carrick makes a violent opposition. I find the farmers object to their children cleaning the schoolroom, and Turner [the agent] thinks they are right, but Mr. Fenwick says it is nonsense, and so I think.

20 October 1843   *Blagdon*

I can give a nice account of Baby, for he seems to have taken a turn, owing apparently to his food having been changed to Tops and Bottoms.[1] He has had two beautiful nights and seems altogether much better. I hope he will now pick up again. It is quite distressing to see him look so small and to feel his little legs so soft and flabby.

Mr. Dawson told me that he thought it very unlikely a wet nurse would suit, so that if he goes on well with the Tops and Bottoms we shall not try one. I fear, too, it might be difficult to manage with Wells. She says the wet nurses never did well where she lived before, and I daresay it was owing to her manner with them. I do better than I did before with her, for I am more decided and not afraid of speaking with her so much as I was. I feel as if the sorrow had given me more strength. You ask about the nurserymaid. I am sorry to say she is going away. I dislike changes so much, but she is not quite strong enough and I am afraid she is rather conceited and given to *giggling*. The little Quiz is coming back, for she is now pronounced by all to be a treasure and is much improved in appearance. I am quite determined not to have two, and indeed I think it is very bad for children to be always waited upon and amused all day, and I would rather little Matt was left to amuse himself on the floor and only watched. It is far better for him than to have a nurse always playing with him. He is with me a great deal, as much as his sleeping and eating and walking will allow, and I always try as much as possible to go on with my occupations and he is generally quite happy.

I see nothing now to prevent our going to Ampthill, and perhaps on the whole I should feel happier that you should not have the long, cold journey, for when you came before I do not think it suited any of you. Besides which, I should find it such a comfort to see dear Ampthill again. Matt says he can very well leave home then, but I will find out *exactly* if he could stay as long as you would stay here before the decision is finally made.

[1] The top and bottom of the loaf, i.e. the hardest crusts, soaked in hot water.

October 1843   *Blagdon*

I do not feel at all inclined to see anyone except Lady Elizabeth Grey, who is away till the end of the month, but I think I shall be obliged to see Mrs. John Cookson. I find she offered as soon as she heard of our distress to come and stay here with her children, which was very kind but I certainly should not have liked it. . . . I hope Papa knows his Godson walked across the room alone yesterday. I was so pleased to see him. He set off with his arms stretched out and ran along till at last he fell. He is very frightened, and indeed I think he is rather a nervous child but so fine and healthy now and so amusing. It is very pretty to see him looking at his little brother, who is always called "wee baby," and playing with his little toes which he admires greatly.

If Charles Ridley is not asked here it will be his own fault. Matt was determined not to consider that he had anything to do with the quarrel. He saw him one day and went to shake hands and welcome him home, and the said Charles put his hands into his pockets, merely said I am very well thank you, and walked away. Is not that a pity?

[Charles was evidently not asked to Blagdon on this occasion. All the brothers must have been in the county at the time, staying perhaps with their sisters, but the others were not so difficult, apparently, for in her next letter Cecilia says:]

William and Henry Ridley are both here now. I like William extremely. He is a kind good-hearted creature with one of the best possible tempers and very affectionate. Poor Henry is quite an invalid and walks lame. He is very funny and very kind. The babes are both well. Little Matt is distressingly shy and in spite of all William's endeavours to make friends he will not go near him, but I hope he will get over it when he is more in the habit of seeing people. Wells does not put Baby into the tub at night but only washes it on her knee. Do you think I ought to make her do otherwise?

[Evidently Lady Parke did not approve of this method of bathing Baby, and the Baron also replied to this letter, saying "I don't mind little Matt being shy: you were so and I am not discontented with you now." Cecilia wrote back:]

Wells does not even wash little Matt in the tub at night. Do you think she ought? I daresay there is no harm in his being shy, but it is always a little disappointment when anyone wishes to see him and he *will* cry the whole time. However, I think that his shyness will not last long. He has made great friends with his Uncle William at last. He really is a nice creature, and though we have not had any conversation directly on the subject I can see how anxious he is to see his mother again and how he despairs of it. I almost despair too now, but yet still I cannot resist hoping that her heart may one day be changed. As far as I can judge, I should really say the daughters behaved very ill, but it is no use talking about that. The only way for it ever to be made up is for both parties to forgive everything. Lady Ridley is now at Yarmouth at a large new hotel there by herself, and I believe she likes it very much. Do you know that she actually had all the schoolroom books and games *burnt*?

I went with William to see one or two of the old women about the place and it was a pleasure to see their delight. There is one nearly ninety years old and she really seemed beside herself when she saw him. She is so attached to the family. She always enquires after all the family and its branches and talks much of that "noble woman Lady Colborne." She was burning some old shoes which perfumed the room very strongly.

William confided to me as a great secret what you tell me about Charles Ridley and I am very sorry for it, but I should not wonder if the marriage some day or other came to pass, for she has, or will have, a good fortune. However, it is a bad thing. Charles seems to have all the susceptibility of the family and to be the only one with rather a fondness for flirting. He has already had many affairs of the kind. When he left England he was desperately in love with Fanny Brandling, and in Canada he lost his heart several times. But I fear this is a more lasting affair, and this distress, together with his great annoyance at not seeing his mother, have made him very wretched.

LITTLE MATT

EDWARD

He and George are gone to winter at Rome. I should like to get them some good introductions but I do not know how.

November 1843   *Blagdon*

I could not find time to write to you yesterday, for I felt so anxious to have as much conversation with Egerton Harcourt as possible.[1] It has been a very great pleasure and comfort to have him here. He is so kind and so full of affection and interest for you all. He came Saturday early and Lady Elizabeth brought him, meaning to sit with me a little on her way to Lambton,[2] but most unfortunately I was out on my pony and missed her. When I got home I found Mrs. John Cookson waiting for me and she staid till late, so that I had very little quiet talk with Egerton, and yesterday William was with me in our walks, so that I could not talk comfortably as I should have liked. But I brought him up into my sitting room to show him the head I have of darling Mary's and one or two other drawings, and then we had some nice quiet talk and I felt it a great comfort. He told me all about you and Charles and talked with such affection of darling Mary that I felt quite to love him for it. I wish he could have staid longer —I might have had more talk with him. I could not help feeling quite to wish William away yesterday, and yet he is such a nice kind creature and takes such care of me when Matt is not there that it was ungrateful to have any such feeling. He knew Mary so very little that I feel my tongue rather tied with him. Egerton said he thought my Baby smaller than dear Mary's, even now, so I fear he must be very wee, but he is well now and as quiet and happy and good as possible. Mr. Dawson says they ought not to be out later than two now, for it always seems rather to change after that. I suppose at Ampthill it is different.

November 1843   *Blagdon*

Yesterday William left us. I walked with him to the coach and

[1] Tenth son of the Archbishop of York and brother of Vernon Harcourt who had wanted to marry Cecilia.

[2] Lambton Castle, Chester le Street, Co. Durham, belongs to the Earl of Durham.

felt quite to lose him. He is such a kind-hearted, amiable creature and though not particularly clever yet he seems to have good sense and a really good heart, and under present circumstances it is a great pleasure to have any of Matt's brothers or sisters here and to be able to show them any kindness.

I believe it is much better for children to be put early into short clothes if they are well, and I should not think there was any risk in doing it in winter, for you can begin by the undergarments and do it by degrees. I was really sorry that the nurserymaid did not turn out quite well, for I should have liked to keep her as you had got her for me, but I fear she is not very steadily disposed. I observed a great deal of forwardness in her manner, and Wells told me that when the doctor came to see her arm she used to be very pert and forward and that she had to find a great deal of fault with her. The one I have got now is a good little active thing. My only fear is that her strength may not be sufficient. Wells makes her carry little Matt all the time he is out and says she could not give the baby to her, but I think that is absurd.

I have got a housemaid very ill now with what Mr. Dawson calls the *green sickness*, which I never heard of before except in the *History of England*.[1]

November 1843   *Blagdon*

I went to Newcastle on Monday to get all my club things. The shop is an excellent one for the purpose, I think, and very cheap. They have nice good blankets at 6/- a pair and I really feel inclined to buy dozens of them, they looked so warm and comfortable. I also had an interview with the schoolmistress and was much pleased with her. She seems a sensible person and apparently well suited for what we want. I should like some hints very much, if you or Charles have any to give, about the rules etc. She is to teach them to sing. I think they should begin every morning with prayers and a hymn, and then read the Bible, and end with prayers. Also I should

---

[1] Green sickness or chlorosis: a form of nutritional anaemia affecting chiefly adolescent girls living in confined conditions.

think if the forenoon were devoted to lessons, the whole afternoon had better be given to work.

[Cecilia's twenty-fourth birthday was on 21 November. A few days beforehand the Baron wrote to Lady Parke:]

I have executed your commission about Cecilia's birthday present. I bought for you at Pickering's Dyce's *Collection of Sonnets*, very handsomely bound for 14/6, and for my present, which Cecilia is to change if she does not like it, Bacon's *Essays*, bound in green morocco. All are to be sent to Newcastle by Pickering's parcel to his correspondents there, either Mr. Charnley or Mr. Currie, booksellers.

[Cecilia thanked him]

a thousand times for the promised books, which will be a great treasure to me. Just what I like best, and most valuable as an offering of your love. Each year as I grow older I feel that my affection for you and dear Mama is greater even than before, and I see more and more how great is the blessing of being your daughter. And now that I have children of my own my great hope and endeavour is—and ever will be—to be to them what you both have been to us, to hold out to them the same example of goodness and unselfishness, to devote myself to them, as you and dear Mama have done ever since I can recollect anything. Such an example is the greatest blessing that a mother can give her child. I never cease to feel its value, but it is almost painful to feel how far I shall fall short of it. This is a melancholy birthday—the anniversary of dear Grandmama's death, and the first I have known without darling Mary's little offering and good wishes. The sadness of the day seems greater when I think of those passed with her when we were in the same room and she used to have her little present at her bedside and give it to me when we first woke.

I really know not what to say as to the time of our going to Ampthill. Matt is very anxious to do what would make us happiest, and he thinks it would be better for us to go to you than for you to come here.

But still there seems to be such a difficulty in leaving his tiresome hounds for more than ten days or a fortnight, which would not be the extent of Papa's spare time I should think. However, I hope there will be a friendly frost to make his presence here unnecessary. It is past twelve, so goodnight.

24 November 1843   *Blagdon*

Yesterday was the Rent Day and the usual dinner in the laundry took place. I went to see it prepared and felt awestruck by the avenue of farmers I had to pass through. There was a goodly display of huge pieces of beef, pies and plum puddings, and the whole affair went off well without any over or under roasting, which often happens. I am afraid, however, the rents were not particularly good.

The Greys are here now, which is very nice. It is delightful having them in this quiet way with no one else, and I cannot say how kind and affectionate and full of feeling she is. It is impossible to have a warmer heart, and, as you have often said, the whole family seem quite remarkable for the same thing. What a blessing it must be to Lady Carlisle to be the mother of so many good and useful people. It is really a blessing to have Lady Elizabeth so near and to think that she is likely to be always there. She is so humble and so quiet that one feels almost surprised as she *opens out* to find the *knowledge* of books and the love of poetry she possesses. We talk constantly together of darling Mary and dear Charles, for whom she evidently feels the deepest affection and anxiety. Mr. Grey is a lively, merry person, very childish and rather boyish both in his appearance and way of talking; extremely fond of novels and not a little so of gossip. But yet at the same time full of anxiety to do good and quite devoted to his church and parish.

November 1843   *Blagdon*

Today I went in the carriage to take my club things to Plessey, and there was a grand distribution there which seemed to please all the people. I went into one cottage where I saw, as I thought, a man sitting by the fire much in need of a clothing fund with nothing on at all. I felt rather astonished and was rather drawing back when the woman explained that it was her boy who had been working in the pit, and I discovered that he was not entirely without clothes for he had an old pair of *breeches* on. Whenever I go to Plessey I am obliged to make a visit to all the people or they are quite jealous. They stand at their doors and call me in, and they begin "Well, Hinny" and tell me all their wants and ailments. There are many nice old women there and all so remarkably clean and tidy—in spite of old age and poverty.

November 1843   *Blagdon*

Here is little Matt playing about, and every now and then giving me a pull, so you must not be surprised at any mistakes. He is very good on the whole, but I cannot do much when he is with me. He can say a few little words and understands all that one says to him. He is in my room when I am dressing every morning and always gives himself a kiss in the long glass. But the prettiest thing is to see him, which very seldom happens, run about with nothing on. He looks such a fat little cherub then. He has just been pushing open the shutters and then came to me with a face full of eagerness and talking in his own way most vehemently. I got up and went to see what it was and I found that it was the moon that delighted him.

The weather is very stormy but quite warm. I rode this morning up to Stannington to pay Mr. Carrick a little account, and whilst I was there there came a tremendous storm of rain, so he offered to hold the horse whilst the groom put on my cloak. But unfortunately the horse began to prance, upon which Mr. Carrick shrieked out loudly and exclaimed that he was terrified to death and wondered that anybody could ever ride. It was really a strange sight—the queer-looking, squinting man pulling at the reins, and I did not wonder at the horse being frightened.

November 1843   *Blagdon*

Tomorrow we are going away for a day or two to suit the hunting in the far country. I am displeased and frightened at the idea of it now that the time has come. But it was a great convenience to Matt and I saw he wished it, and I thought of what Charles said, that one should not live for oneself but for others, so I consented, and now I do not know whether I was right. Wells is in a heavenly temper. It is such a comfort to feel such confidence when one leaves the babes.

I have just got your dear letter. . . . I feel that I cannot think too much or dwell too incessantly on our sorrow. It must be intended that we should do so, and certainly it cannot be right to strive to forget or to deaden the grief that God sends us. I often am quite astonished to think how I can go on as I did before about my daily occupations, and how I can be cheerful as I am, and I *almost*, indeed I often, quite fancy it is wrong. Partly, I think, it is constitutional, for I think the joy or sorrow of my heart does not often appear outwardly, and partly the calmness I feel owing to your example.

[Lady Parke replied from Ampthill:]

I daresay your change of air and of scene will have done you good. I am sure it is right you should go and it is good for Sir Matthew to do so, darling, and as you say this makes no real difference in one's feelings, for our thoughts are ever occupied with the past, and yet we must not make those about us suffer for our sorrow . . .

I am driven into a corner, as Papa would say, for I have had the Rector to dine and he dawdled on until it is too near post time, so I must scribble as fast as my pen will go . . . I am very busy with all sorts of things—teaching children and talking about plants and pasting up holes and corners, but in order to keep out the wind this house would be lined with paper and every joint stuffed with tow. I hope it will not take fire, for it would burn very quickly . . . I have a beautiful Blagdon geranium here and I can give you a very pretty sort we have here that I think you will like. I feel as if the time will go sadly too fast while you are here, but I must not spoil the happiness of having you by dwelling upon that. I know the hourly comfort now of looking forward to it, and I can hope and trust that nothing may come to prevent such a happening. Adieu, my own dear child, you are very dear to me and I still have much to be grateful for in having you. God bless and protect you and ever let me be your affectionate mother,   C. Parke.

December 1843   *Blagdon*

Dearest Mama, Do you know it was really a relief to me to find that
you thought that I had done right in going from home, as I felt uncomfortable in doing so. We came home today from the Bells.
Everyone was very kind indeed and Mrs. Bell particularly so. Indeed
she always is and seems to take an interest in me. She has beautiful
flowers and a comfortable old house and a large affectionate family
circle which I always like to see. I went this morning from there to
see Mrs. John Cookson and lunch with her, and next week we are
going there for two nights. She has a fine healthy baby of four months
old which she is nursing with great success, drinking only water and
getting to a size unequalled in the present day. I often wish she
was a little different, for although very amiable and estimable she is
not quite the companion I should like. She is an excellent mother
and wife and has a patience and unselfishness that one must admire,
but she is altogether devoid of all charm of mind and taste and soul,
which I have always so loved and which was so remarkable in our
sweet Mary. I shall always recollect that dear Mary did not fancy
her at all. Mrs. E. Ogle suits me much better. Mary was much
pleased with her and I have really felt a comfort in seeing her lately
and can even talk to her as I can to few people. I do not know why
it is, but I feel that she understands me and feels for me.

[On 8 December the Baron wrote to Cecilia from Ampthill:]

My darling Child, What a love you are to write so kindly, so agreeably
and so frequently to your old Papa, and that without a reciprocity
treaty. I have not been able to write to you as often as I ought and
as you deserve. After a great hurry and skurry I contrived to get to
the railroad station, on Wednesday, just, and only just, in time to
come here by the last train, in my own carriage, where there was
barely room to sit without moving, such was the quantity of interior
baggage of all descriptions. Books, wig boxes, ham, cheese, wine,
papers; for the use of the circuit and the mansion here, which is
voted at present to have a very deficient library, and which we must
supply with a little winter cheer for our expected and much loved

guests. I found your dearest Mama well, though I think she a little overfatigues herself. Alice quite well and the baby in excellent health and beauty. I should be delighted if you brought both your darlings to be its companions, and do not think of leaving them at home from any fear that they would not be most welcome guests.

I have been to see the bust of our beloved Mary twice at Lough's.[1] The likeness cannot well be more perfect and the look is sweet and intelligent. But there is, or was, when I saw it, something wanting to make it what one wished—something of elegance and refinement. It had rather an air of *dowdiness* which occasionally, in her moments of perfect ease and negligence, she put on. But I have suggested some alterations which will go far to remove this, and then it will, I hope, do credit to, and be of great use to, poor Lough. How dearly I value that once worthless and despised daguerreotype! I see now, whenever I please to use a magnifying glass, her beauteous face, with an air of thoughtful sweetness, which makes all the charms of her countenance. My sight and memory assist each other and I behold your lovely sister again!

I want to beg a Xmas box from you. My fox's brush has become the prey of other useless animals, and is a sad memento of the power of moths. So if Matt is successful enough to kill another before Christmas, bring it with you, dear . . . Adieu, dearest child.

December 1843   *Blagdon*

Dearest Papa, We had a most melancholy letter from the Loughs yesterday. I do not know whether they wish the state of their affairs to be a secret or not, but I cannot help thinking that some of the great and rich people of the world would be very likely to give him orders if they knew what a state he is in. They said yesterday they were

[1] John Lough, the Newcastle sculptor (1798–1876), was generously patronised by Sir Matthew who spent many thousands of pounds on his works. These included many of the characters in Shakespeare, as well as most Classical and Biblical figures and duplicate portraits of all the family. They now adorn the grounds at Blagdon but have not proved such an investment as Sir Matthew hoped when he commissioned them.

positively so reduced that he had to go out and see if he could borrow a few pounds to pay his men, and that he had only eighteen shillings in the world. Literally now he lives upon what he gets from Matt, who pays him every now and then as much as he can, and Lough hurries on his things much more than we wish really because he has no other hope. It is very sad. I cannot bear to think of it for he is so excitable and I should never be surprised at his going out of his mind.

[To Cecilia's appeal on Lough's behalf the Baron replied:]

I think it better not to disclose generally Lough's condition, for no one employs an artist at a high rate from charity. I am sorry for him. He is a man of genius, undoubtedly; but he is proud and somewhat self sufficient, and dare not conciliate. How odd that he should not have set about dear Mary's bust immediately that I asked him in August, considering what state his affairs were.

[Cecilia answered:]

I hope Lough will make a satisfactory bust of Mary. You are quite right in all you say of him, though I cannot but feel very much for him. He has the consciousness of great genius, of the capability of executing great works, and yet he has constantly before his eyes the fear of utter ruin to himself and his children and wife. He no doubt thinks more highly of himself than he ought, and sets a higher value upon *genius* than it has, and he has not firmness of mind and principle to struggle against the trials that weigh down upon him. His wife, too, makes him worse, for she has the same excitable nature and not very well regulated mind, with a great contempt—not only for other artists—but for everyone who does not appreciate his works as she thinks they ought to be. They often make me rather indignant by little instances of false pride and by the excessive admiration he has for his own talents, but yet I do feel that his is a hard lot and one which many would sink under. Matt says the usual custom is to pay £50 when the bust is done in the clay, and the other £50 when the

C.R.—K

marble is completed. It will be a great comfort if he succeeds in making a good likeness and I really believe he will try to do so. He always seemed very grateful to you and Mama.

[Lough evidently did succeed in making a good likeness of Mary, for in the spring of 1844 it was exhibited at the Royal Academy where Cecilia saw it. She describes it in the only surviving letter written from London:]

I had just time to swallow some lunch when Lady Ridley arrived. She looked remarkably well, much *beflounced* and very smart. Matt and I went later with her to the Royal Academy, only into the bust room, and there I saw dear Mary. I did not go close to it or examine it, for I really felt it impossible, and indeed I could hardly venture to look much at it, it seemed to me to be herself, her own dear darling face.

CHAPTER THIRTEEN

Spring 1844

MATT and Cecilia went to Ampthill for Christmas 1843, returning to Blagdon about the middle of January. Cecilia became pregnant about this time, and on coming home she wrote to her mother:

Yesterday I had two very long walks and was not in the slightest degree tired. Indeed I feel quite different now to what I was before I went to Ampthill and am as strong as I could wish. Indeed I think I am getting quite fat. I am just going to set out to go first to the school and then to Morpeth and see if Lady Elizabeth will drive with me to pay a visit—perhaps to Lady Mary Monck if there is time. Wee Baby is much better today. I fear, however, he is a delicate child. Little Matt is in high force and very merry.

I am deeply interested in Prescott and very glad I made myself a present of it.[1] I am afraid we cannot use your ham receipt, for we have no smoking house.

January 1844   *Blagdon*

Yesterday I went with Lady Elizabeth to Belsay. It was a stormy day and we were a long time making up our minds whether or not it was fit to go, but at last we took the brave line and went, and I enjoyed the drive with her extremely. We were rather too late in our operations and when we arrived we found Lady Mary's coach at the door and the ladies all cloaked and furred ready for a drive. However, we could not go straight back on account of the horses, so we got out. Then there was an affair of luncheon, slow in coming and slow in ending, and afterwards they were an immense time bringing

[1] *History of the Conquest of Mexico* by W. H. Prescott (1843).

the carriage, and all the time the *wrapt up* ladies sat there, waiting and no doubt feeling very angry at us. I did not get home until near six, but happily the shutters were in a good humour and closed beautifully.

I suppose you have not yet had time to read *Mexico*? I find it very interesting but am shocked to find that my sympathy *will* go along with Cortes, contrary to all that is right and proper and usual.

Lady Ashbrook and her daughter[1] have offered to come and stay with us in a day or two on their way from Scotland. I shall not at all object to having them.

28 January 1844   *Blagdon*

I believe the cause of your not hearing from me on Friday was *cowardice*, for I had forgotten my letter until I was getting into bed; so I sallied forth to get it and put it into the box, but my courage failed, for I knew the gentlemen were not gone to bed and I was afraid of meeting them. So after some minutes of irresolution I threw the letters downstairs and left them to their fate.

We have only the Burrells to meet Lady Ashbrook. The Brandlings have at present a house full of company—in short we have no hope of anyone now. It is wonderful how difficult it is to collect a party.

February 1844   *Blagdon*

Lady Ashbrook is here. Very important, fat and talky and full of self, and her daughter, Charlotte Flower, just the reverse—a nice, gentle, quiet, modest girl. I like her and her drawings much, but Lady A. is rather too much for me. Her favourite topic is her own *confinements* and sufferings. She has been playing the harp quite *beautifully*, it is quite a treat. We were quite alone tonight and shall be tomorrow, but I hope for some people on Monday. Last night did very well. Lady A. knew Mrs. Burrell's mother and they both had

[1] Emily Theophilia, daughter of Sir Thomas Metcalfe, Bart., married in 1812, as his second wife, Viscount Ashbrook. Charlotte Augusta was their only daughter and she married in 1846 the fifth Duke of Marlborough, as his second wife.

been much abroad and talked it all over, and Miss Flower would do with anyone. They stay till Wednesday.

Tuesday, February 1844 *Blagdon*

Lady Ashbrook is still here and alas, in spite of all our endeavours, there is no one to meet her. We have asked such numbers of people, it is quite curious. I think her remarkably disagreeable, and her daughter remarkably the reverse. Only fancy her beginning to tell me about Lord Ashbrook! She certainly does play most delightfully on the harp. She composes as she plays and her touch is wonderful. It is quite a treat to hear her. Charlotte Flower has a great taste for drawing, particularly boats, and she is a very nice girl, so sensible and unselfish and pleasing altogether. Little Matt is so good and much less shy and he has quite taken a fancy to Miss F., but shrinks from Lady A., which I do not wonder at.

Wednesday, February 1844 *Blagdon*

I am so thankful Lady Ashbrook is gone. She is really not nice, but at the same time I like Miss Flower so much that she made up for Mama. They both sent many messages to you. They seem to have an immense acquaintance and Lady A. is always talking of Hamilton Palace and the Princess Maria[1] who is a great friend of Miss F.'s. I suppose it is for her sake that people tolerate her mother. She never listens to anything that anybody says and is so conceited about her music.

February 1844 *Blagdon*

I think you would quite get over Charlotte Flower's *doddy doddy* look if you saw much of her. I really began quite to admire her and wondered how I could have thought her plain. She is particularly agreeable and has such a pleasing voice, and evidently such a wish that others should be pleased, that it gives her a great charm. I feel as if I had been rather hard on Lady Ashbrook, for after all she was on the whole very good natured and seemed quite happy without company and just as willing to play as if there were many listeners. One day,

[1] A Princess of Baden, who married the Duke of Hamilton.

unfortunately, Dr. and Mrs. Headlam were here. Lady A. sat down with great pomp and played her best and stopped, expecting great applause. But Dr. Headlam was asleep and Mrs. H. only said "How pretty!" This was a sad disappointment and I had to use all my arts of persuasion to induce her to play again. She has great execution and great expression, but I should say not much feeling—indeed how could she?

We have just been up to the school and found it going on well. Miss Potts (the *French* young lady) has given up coming to school because I would not allow her to come with long gold earrings. I think she is better away. I am going to have the girls taught to work in a new way, beginning with canvas and coloured thread. I want to bring up the little ones to be good workers—it is hopeless with the big ones.

16 February 1844   *Blagdon*

I have an important event to tell you, for the Wee Baby was christened yesterday. Old Mr. Myers christened him, and the Burrells were here. I was afraid of the cold snow but there was a thaw. Baby re-entered his long clothes for the day in order to wear the beautiful robe that is kept for the occasion and which he has almost outgrown now. It is a foolish thing, a vast of money, but very pretty of its kind. He was as good as possible, quite quiet and looked very grave as if he knew it was a solemn thing. Little darling, he really looks so pretty and so lively and seems so well now, it is quite delightful.

Only think how odd: I suppose Lady Ridley is offended at something. She has never answered my last two letters and I had not the slightest idea she was going to Brighton. I do not think I shall write again unless she does.

February 1844   *Blagdon*

I see a storm coming on Wells's countenance and I am meditating a scold, for she has given little Matt castor oil without asking. I think she said little M. is very restless and rather irritable in general. Sometimes he is very good, but I generally find him in the nursery in a whining state, which must proceed from bad management. Mrs.

Burrell's children are in beautiful order and always so nicely dressed and clean, and she only has one nurse for the three, and there are only eleven months between two of them, and she never had more than one nurse, and that is generally the case about here, and I really think it is far better for the children than to be too much fussed after. I do not think I shall have an extra nurserymaid when I have three children. I shall not require any work to be done, for that can be done at the school, and no cleaning. I hope therefore to have a nice comfortable nurse with good sense and a good temper. I should like to enquire in Yorkshire, but I am afraid of trusting Aunt Fanny. I am determined not to have a London nurse if I can help it.

1 March 1844   *Blagdon*

Dearest Papa, I suppose you are now on the circuit, but at what place I do not exactly know. I wish it had been Newcastle, but however that is to be in the summer . . . Matt went in this morning to be on the Grand Jury and was to dine in Newcastle, and I have had what Lady Ashbrook calls a *severe tea* and am now sitting alone and expecting him to return. We had some fears, a day or two ago, that we should not be able to lead coals in the snow, and therefore we diminished our fires and are now living only in the library and the hall, which I think very snug and comfortable.

There is a great excitement going on in the county in the formation of an *Anti-Corn Law League,* and our old friend Mr. Burrell has been exerting himself immensely for it. I wonder if it is a right and lawful thing, for it strikes me as rather doubtful and rather useless. There seems to be something of the sort in most counties now and sometimes it leads to violent abuse of the opposite party, which seems to me undignified. There was a great meeting today at Morpeth of all the gentlemen and tenants who are against free trade in corn. They assembled in great numbers and agreed to form an association, and although it was agreed that the meeting should have nothing to do at all with politics and make no allusion to the measures of any Government, yet Mr. Liddell made a long, foolish speech saying that Sir Robert Peel should be supported etc. and thereby annoyed his hearers very much. Matt told him afterwards that he really had *bored* them all very much. I wonder if he will be offended at such a rude speech, but he seems to be a foolish person and to have won anything but golden opinions from all sorts of men. Matt brought home six gentlemen to dine—only think how overpowering.

Little Matt can now say Papa and Mama and makes attempts at various other words but not always with success. I was in hopes he had quite got over his shyness, but today he came down to see Mrs. Ogle and the moment he was in the room there was such a tremendous roar that I was quite overpowered and obliged to dismiss him immediately. I hope you will not have any lumbago or gout on the circuit. I do not know who your brother Judge is, or your Marshal.

2 March 1844   *Blagdon*

Dearest Mama, Little Matt is becoming very amusing and is just now very good and very merry, and so is Wee Baby. I cannot bear letting them stay so much in the house, but I follow your advice and do not insist against Wells, so I hope they will not suffer from it. I only am afraid of tendering them and I cannot help thinking that a strong boy like little Matt would be better for going out in the frosty air. Wells is quite shocked at the idea of his going without a frock in his blouse and thinks it, I suppose, a fresh proof of stinginess . . . But she is in rather a good humour now and I do not think she means to go herself. She is certainly better than she was, since I have had more of a will and has not ventured to speak as she used to do, but I do not feel altogether on comfortable terms with her—there is a sort of restraint which is unpleasant.

March 1844   *Blagdon*

Wells I found very grave and *uncommunicative*, which I attributed at first to a very bad account of her brother she had just had. However, yesterday the truth came out—that it was all because I had left a book with her to read. I had not finished it myself till just before I went away when I gave it to her, and unfortunately she found in it a sheet of paper on which I had written a few Madame *Neckerish* remarks about babies, all of which she took as aimed at herself and was deeply offended, said no one else in the house had books left them in that way, etc., etc., and in short we had quite an *explication très vive*. I certainly blame myself for leaving the paper in the book, but it shows how very thin-skinned and ridiculous she is. I find so many things I want to talk over, and we must do so when we meet. I feel as if I wanted so much advice about my children.

March 1844   *Blagdon*

I can give you a very good report of us all here. We have had a mild day and I have been both driving and walking, but the latter is a very dirty occupation now and makes one long for stilts. I gener-ally come home ankle-deep in mud. . . . Little Matt has been ordered to have leather boots to support his ankle, and the old shoe-maker in the village has made a little pair of boots very tidily but so stiff that I am afraid little Matt can hardly walk in them. I went today to try and persuade him to take the stiffening out, which seemed greatly to annoy him, as he said it was the chief beauty of them.

There is very little out yet in the garden—only snowdrops and hepaticas, and crocuses there will be soon, and double violets. I am going to write to Carter's for seeds in a day or two. Do you think an Irish family is a bad place to take a cook from? We are going to have a pair of storks on our pond, and I hear that squirrels will do very well here, so I hope you will give us a pair in the summer.

[I imagine Cecilia wanted a pair of grey squirrels, since the red have always been indigenous at Blagdon, where are still quantities of them. The grey squirrel has not yet reached Northumberland. They were first introduced into England by the Duke of Bedford at his zoo at Woburn, so that it would have been easy for Lady Parke to have got a pair.

The next two letters are from the Baron to Cecilia.]

March 1844   *Stafford*

It is a great shame, I own it, that I have not sooner written to you, my darling, and thanked you for your kind, and always most welcome and agreeable letters: but I have been busy, pretty generally, and rather indolent in an evening, and very early in bed. I hope I shall improve. In point of health, I may say *par parenthèse*, I never was better, or indeed so well, on any circuit: moderate work, temperance and a little quiet exercise, have produced this result. Our circuit has been cheerful and diversified: and we have had so many different things to do, that it seems like a quarter of a year since I left my home and its dear tenants. First I went to the quiet town and moderate labours of Abingdon—diversified by two very agreeable visits to Nuneham,[1] where there was a large family party: and Georgiana was very kind, and almost affectionate, if I may use the term. Then came the gravities of Oxford: with its sombre antiquities, and learned and courteous dons, and young noblemen in their gawdy gowns, and much quiet hospitality. This was followed by the grandeurs of Blenheim, now beginning to shine forth again, in its old splendour, by means of some £25,000 which the Duke is now dispensing upon it. Here we spent a day, that is dined, slept and breakfasted. His Grace gave a great feast to the gentry of Oxfordshire, to meet the Judges, and was very hospitable and courteous. He drank nothing but toast and water, which is, *on dit*, the direct opposite of what he has done before. Lord Blandford was there: and Sir James South[2], who had come down to assist the young Marquis in his astronomical pursuits, he having, very happily, a taste for discovering the heavenly bodies, which had descended to him from his great grandfather. They set to work in the morning to find spots in the sun, which neither I nor Sir James South could discover, but the young aspirant could: and he turned out to be right. When after my return to town there is any curious phenomenon to be seen, some remarkable double stars, or Jupiter in full force at a convenient time, or Venus crescent, Sir James is to let me know, and I am to go and peep through his celebrated glass. Would you like to go too?

After Blenheim came the hardish work of Worcester. I slept a night

[1] Nuneham Courtenay, near Oxford, described in *Paterson's Roads* as the "magnificent seat of the Earl of Harcourt."

[2] Sir James South (1785–1867), astronomer; observed in London with Sir John Herschel and in Paris with Laplace. Knighted 1830.

at Birmingham, after the tempestuous rocking of a railroad, such as
I never experienced before, and never wish to experience again. In
the morning early I went to Wolverhampton—then to Hilton . . .
and slept there and came here the next morning, where I have disposed of all my own business and part of Coleridge's in less than three
days, the usual time for the transaction whereof is a week. I am now
on the point of going by railroad to Whitmore, thence by carriage to
Drayton, by horse to Hawkston, Lord Hill's, where I am to dine and
sleep and walk about tomorrow and thence to Shrewsbury! Here is
variety.

March 1844.   *Hawkston,[1] Monmouth Circuit*

After dinner we adjourned to a drawing room, covered with gild-
ing, having previously sat round a fire in the dining room, with a
crescent of a table and a set of screens intervening, so that your eyes
were not dazzled, but your feet were well warmed by the fire, and the
bottles circulated, by means of a mechanical contrivance, a souvenir
of old times when people used to drink—happily they are old times,
and I hope will never be renewed. About half past nine we all went
to a very nice chapel, where, as on every evening and morning, a
chaplain read a chapter of scripture and a prayer, and all the family,
guests and servants attended—the two former in a gallery, the latter
in pews. Yesterday after breakfast I took a ride with Lord Hill over
the park. If the weather had been fine it would have been the most
beautiful ride in England. For wood, water, cultivated fields and its
varied mountain outline, I could not conceive any more striking—but
the distant view, which I had partly seen the day before, was obscured
by mist, and I was left in a great measure to conjecture what its
beauties were, as seen from the terrace at Hawkston. Lord Hill is
obviously a very good country gentleman. My Lady has a pretty face,
and is like a little bird—is shy, but I believe very amiable and good,
and a great patroness of schools for the poor, so I readily forgive her
for supposing I had travelled the circuit for fifty years.

[1] Hawkston, in Shropshire, belonged to the second Viscount Hill, Lord-
Lieutenant of the county. He married in 1831 Anne, only child of
Joseph Clegg of Peplow Hall, Salop.

17 March 1844   *Blagdon*

Dearest Mama, We are quite starved here—snow thick on the ground
and a piercing wind, quite a second edition of winter which we hoped
had gone. I was so glad to receive your letter yesterday, and also one
from dear Papa giving me a charming account of his circuit, which
seems to have been very agreeable to him. I think it is a promising
trait in Lord Blandford to be fond of astronomy.

. . . When the children cannot go out I always make them come
down to the drawing room for the time they would have been out, to
have a good walk through the rooms, and generally I make Wells come
with them, but today I found her looking so unhappy and miserable
that I brought them both down and left her to have a little time to
herself. They were both very merry and Baby quite delighted to
have a little run, and I always enjoy having them much more if Wells
is not there.

Tell me what to do. Mr. Dawson says still I had better try to nurse
and that he has no doubt I shall be able, and that at any rate I ought
to do it for the first six weeks for my own sake, and longer if I find it
suit. Do you think I had better decide upon having a wet nurse after
the first six weeks, and get him to look out for one before, or had I
better leave it till I see how it does? I am very well and can walk
better than I could a short time ago. On some days I am soon tired
but on most days I have a very fair walk twice and feel quite brisk
and well all day. My back is very much better on the whole and I
hope you are well yourself, dearest Mama. You never say whether
you are.

23 March 1844   *Blagdon*

I must tell you about my visit to Mrs. Coulson.[1] We came back
yesterday, and on Friday I had a nice drive with her through a very
wild country—moorland and rock with the river Coquet running
through it. It was a beautiful morning and the lights on the hills
were very good. Cheviot looked very well covered with snow. Mrs.

[1] Daughter of the seventh Lord Byron, nephew of the poet. She
married, as his second wife, John Blenkinsopp Coulson of Blenkinsopp
Castle.

Coulson is very delicate in consequence of having been much mis-managed in one of her confinements by a village doctor, and she now cannot walk and is obliged always to drive. She is a very pleasing, ladylike person, remarkably so, and I am very glad to have made more acquaintance with her. You would not recognise in her the little slim, shy looking girl we met at the Carltons', for she is grown immensely fat. She has six fine boys, all so well mannered and tractable that I think she must have brought them up very well.

Do tell me your advice respecting the cow I asked you about.

April 1844   *Blagdon*

Little Matt is troubled with his eye teeth and had a very restless night. Wells watched him the whole night and I believe hardly went to bed at all. She is very valuable in that respect, but I could not help feeling angry at her when I went upstairs after dinner and she said so much about his being in such a fever and so ill, and that she was sure he was going to be very bad, so that if I was disposed to be nervous and fidgetty she would drive me mad. I wonder, after that, I am so little so, but in spite of all she said his face and hands were as cool and comfortable as possible, so that I should not admit any of her terrors. I have made up my mind not to keep her another year, for though she has many virtues and is certainly a clever nurse, she does not suit me and takes too much upon herself.

April 1844   *Blagdon*

Just a line today, for I am afraid you will be anxious about little Matt. He had a quiet good night and is certainly better. Mr. Dawson has been here and says he is going on quite well, though he is very irritable this morning and feels uncomfortable from the effects of a dose of calomel last night. He has had no attack in his breathing since yesterday morning, and I hope he may soon be quite well again, but we must watch him carefully for a long time and be always on our guard. Mr. Dawson says he will get the better of it entirely with care. The weather is so very warm that I find it quite oppressive and can hardly bear to stay in the nursery, where they cannot open the windows whilst little Matt is in the room. It makes me feel quite faint, which is very unlucky. Little Matt was sleeping so quietly last night that I did not take Baby down. Wells shines in a case like this. She is so patient and one would think she had the most perfect temper in the world. She watches everything so well, and really it is a comfort to be able to trust so in her now, for I feel that I myself could not be more careful. Besides which—though I am very well— I soon get very tired and faint with carrying Baby about.

April 1844 *Blagdon*

Yesterday I had a letter from you . . . You are very good to think about another nurse for me but I really fear I could not manage it— it would lead to much grumbling and bother, for Wells certainly is an irritable person. I have talked much to her about getting Mrs. Ramsay, but she would not hear of it, and I thought on the whole it would cause more trouble than it would avoid, and would not make much difference to Wells in point of rest. Wee Baby is not at all neglected, little darling. If I thought he was, I would not mind Wells's furies but have another directly. He is to begin broth today. Sir John Fife thinks he is very like Papa. I think he has a very happy disposition. Have no fears for me. I am very well, take great care of myself and have great care taken of me.

Sunday, 14 April 1844 *Blagdon*

I have not been to church this morning but hope to go in the afternoon. The babies had a bad night and little Matt had a very sharp attack again this morning. Mr. Dawson has not yet been here. I think the rather damp afternoon yesterday may have caused this. They were not out, but I had them both in the drawing room to run about, and perhaps it was not so warm as the nursery. Baby is very well and lively this morning, but I fear—poor little darling—he will not get on well now, and indeed I am sure he is rather smaller in the last few days. How I wish they could be out like your darling all day and dipped into cold water, but now they say the slightest cold or damp air would be so very bad for them. Baby has broth now and sucks it out of his bottle with tops and bottoms in it. The doctors say little Matt must not sit in a basket on the donkey, but have a pad and learn to sit astride, so I have ordered the said pad.[1]

Concerning pelisses, I have had little Matt's blue one turned, and Baby has got a white merino one made out of the white cloak which there was no prospect of using much, and they look very tidy and will do until we go to town, when I must have some of your advice upon the important subject.

April 1844   *Blagdon*

Mr. Dawson told me the other day that he thought a healthy strong child should never be nursed more than seven months. He recommends that some kind of farinaceous food should be mixed with the broth, which he says makes it more wholesome, and now he says we must give Baby a little gravy every day or let him suck a piece of meat, and that by this diet we shall avoid the risk of his nerves getting out of order in teething. Wells has given up the bottle and feeds him entirely with the spoon. I do hope that little Matt will perhaps be better after this, for I have never felt quite happy about his crying so often and being so restless. Wells certainly is as careful as possible, but I have a sort of idea that her nervousness of manner and excitability may be catching to a child. Certainly he does not inherit nervousness from *me*, for I seem to myself to have no nerves, at least now. Only fancy, the other night, when she thought it was croup, her beginning to describe all the horrors of it and the consequences afterwards, and then adding "but they very seldom recover at all."

April 1844   *Blagdon*

I told Aunt Fanny that since little Matt's illness I had determined, for the present at any rate, to put up with inconvenience and keep Wells, for she really has some qualities which are very valuable to me. This morning we had the doctors and we had a long consultation as to the management we were to continue of little Matt, and it so happened that after this consultation they had no talk with Wells, which caused her to be exceedingly grumpy all the morning, but towards

[1] He was only eighteen months old.

afternoon it went off. She likes to talk with the doctors and receive instructions straight from them and not through me, which is one of her weaknesses. Sir John Fife says that he has no doubt at all that his little patient will be in all respects right, and he dwells on the moral treatments of letting him see people and things and urging him to active amusements—in short rousing and leading him on in all ways. Yesterday, acting upon this principle, I took him to Morpeth to have his hair cut, and altogether it was a ridiculous affair. I stopt at the Rectory to ask which was the best hair cutter, and then drove there and found that the man was gone to shave a gentleman. However, they sent for him, and he soon appeared, but he had such a little hot shop with so many children about that I made him go into the inn and sent Wells there with little Matt, and as I had not taken the nurserymaid, I staid in the carriage with Baby. After a while I got out and took Baby in and found poor little Matt in a perfect agony and the little barber in despair. However, the hair was cut and before we got home it was all right.

April 1844   *Blagdon*

Today has been quite lovely and we have all been out nearly all day. The pad being finished, the donkey was brought and Little Matt had his first interview with it, but could not be persuaded to mount for more than a minute. Matt rode it about and we put Baby on and then fed the donkey and used all our arts to entice the young gentleman, but he was rather awestruck today, as I expected he would be, and we must accomplish it by slow degrees. He is very small to ride in such a manner, but as the doctors both of them say so much about it, we must try. He has been yesterday and today so much more gay and happy, it is very encouraging. I shall be very glad, however, not to hear the sort of petted cry which is so frequent, but I must be patient, and it is astonishing what an assistance it is to look upon all these things as a part of our education for another life. Sir John Fife is quite enchanted with Baby and so is Mr. Dawson, and Baby always looks so pleased with them. They say it is a great thing for little Matt to have such a brother with such a happy disposition.

Matt thinks the best way to send the squirrels would be to send them by the carrier from Ampthill to a wharfinger, and for them to come down in charge of a captain of a steamer, if that would not be troublesome to you, and tomorrow I can send the name of the wharf. I do not know what *Honesty* is—how odd that sounds.

April 1844   *Blagdon*

We are quite happy now about the babies. They are both so much better . . . We persuaded little Matt yesterday to mount the donkey for about half a minute, but not without great lamentations. Baby sits on it most manfully. I think we may now look forward to going south the first week in May. I cannot say how I delight in the idea of being at Ampthill, and I think it would do the chicks so much good. Matt said you were very kind about it, but as we were only in town for a short time he thought we should not be able to go backwards and forwards much. I shall not like being in town without you.

I will see about the camellia seeds. It is a very slow, uncertain business I believe, and the best plan would be to buy a few plants. A few go a great way. My gardener says that *Lunaria* is the proper name for *Honesty* and that it is a British flower. You surpass us in roses very much and violets too. Our violets are very plentiful and handsome, but I think they have a bad smell. I think I have nearly driven the gardener out of his mind by the alterations in the flower garden. Yesterday he looked so despairing that I could hardly bring myself to talk to him about it. He has no taste and does not enter into our views, and he suggests things which we do not agree to, and then he is rather stupid in drawing out the shapes and I cannot get him to see when they are right. However, as far as we have gone, I feel quite satisfied and think it will look very well.

April 1844   *Blagdon*

You are a wonderful person to be up so early and do so much. I wish I was like you. I feel as if I was so idle and inactive when I think of you. I am very late now in the morning generally—at least not by any means early. Do you think little Matt could sleep in a

C.R.—L

small bed in London or must he have a crib? Do you mean Baby to have a Leghorn hat and feather? What should little Matt have by way of a hat or cap?

I meant to go today to Newcastle, but there is such a hurricane that I doubt whether it will be safe to go.

Later. I have been to Newcastle, been nearly blown away and done all my shopping. I am very tired—I had so much walking, and the wind to contend with as well. Perhaps by tomorrow we shall have made up our minds touching the journey. I really do rather dread going so far with the chicks and often wish I was going to stay and *you all* coming here instead.

April 1844   *Blagdon*

A day or two ago Wells asked me if I would raise her wages. I was taken by surprise and said I would consider, and yesterday evening, after having consulted long with Matt, I decided NO, and went upstairs to tell her, but I found her in such grief that I could not say anything to her about it. She had just had a very bad account of her brother, who seems to be in the last stage of consumption and rapidly sinking. She was in very great distress—said he was her favourite brother and seemed so grieving at not being able to go to him, which I fear is impossible, as he lives near London. I felt so sorry for her, poor thing. What do you think about the wages? It seems to me very early for her to ask for an increase, and I meant to say to her that I was not inclined at present to give her more. Surely twenty guineas is enough? We suspected that it was intended as a sort of trial to see whether I wished to keep her or not, and it is really a very important question to decide. She has so many excellent qualities and is so trustworthy and so devoted to her duties and is certainly clever in managing their health, that if I thought she would be good for the children in other respects, I would not mind her being disagreeable to me—at least I ought not, but I cannot help thinking that it must be bad for them to be with a person whose temper is not good, and she is not sensible about many things. She had a great deal of talk about the book which had so offended her. She said if I would only tell her anything myself.

26 April 1844 *Blagdon*

We think of going on May 6th or 7th and I think we shall stop at Ampthill for a wee visit—two or three nights I mean, which will be very delightful. Will you tell me, dearest Mama, what you mean to do about Alice's mourning? Merely because I must arrange what I take to town accordingly. I suppose we had best continue some months.[1]

Today we have had an arrival in the shape of a *deer*—a real one from Trondheim which we have fed upon lichen. It is a most curious looking creature and perfectly tame.

28 April *Blagdon*

Thank you for your advice about the nursing. We will talk it over when we meet, and as it is most probable that I shall have a wet nurse I should not want another nurserymaid till she was gone. The fact is that the custom of the country here is to give low wages and to have few servants, so that I feel always as if it was foolish to do more than my neighbours. Particularly as I think we live too extravagantly and we must have a much less expensive cook, for really it will not do to go on as we have done. We must try to get a good cook without so much pretension and I must keep a tight hand over her. I often wish we had not such a large house in town—it entails so much expense and so many servants and does not add a bit to one's happiness. However, we have got it, so I must only look at the good side of it, and it is certainly an enjoyable house. It was all that ridiculous Lady Ridley who caused such outgoings and put all things into a style that requires such expense, and that is not easy to alter, and it was just of a piece with all her character. I do not mean to say that we overspend, but that what with the younger children's fortunes and other outgoings, we live quite to the extent of our income, and as the family increases more expense must be necessary. All this must be very tiresome to you, and I do not know why I say it, for I think we have often talked it over. I am sure you will think I am right in principle. . . . I went out in the middle of this and met Henry Ridley on the road, who was coming to take his chance of

[1] It was now eight months since Mary's death.

finding us to send away a dull fit he had. He looks very well and no thinner.

I am so happy at the thought of being at Ampthill for a few days. How delightful it will be. I think perhaps the room I had, or Matt's dressing room, would be best for the chicks—only you have perhaps made the beds too nice. I am afraid you will be taking a great deal of trouble about arranging for them, but I think I recollect there was a crib, and if that could be put by the large bed, Baby could sleep in it, and little Matt in the bed with Wells, and you could put Bella with Heseltine or one of the housemaids. Or if you are arranging the crib for your pet, both my babies could sleep in the large bed, and Wells on a sofa in the room. I only hope you will not give yourself any trouble.

May 1844   *Blagdon*

I am rather in a state of confusion today, making arrangements for things during our absence, so I feel as if I should certainly have forgotten half, in spite of my pains. We have a beautiful day, but the glass is falling and I am not very sanguine about tomorrow. It will be a long journey for the children and I shall make them set off very early, and we must follow as soon as we can and perhaps make use of the railroad for ourselves. Baby is so extremely brown now that I am quite distressed, for he will not be in beauty. He is quite altered by it and the journey will tan him still more, so that he will really not look pretty. Little Matt is getting too fat and he now *waddles* so dreadfully that Papa will certainly christen him the *Major*. I am afraid he will not make himself agreeable at Ampthill at all. He screams and cries most awfully at the sight of a stranger or the sound of a strange voice, but he looks the picture of health now. Will he require the same kind of hat as last year or not? It seems to me more meant for a baby in arms than for one that walks. Wells is in despair that Wee Baby has *no* hat. There was a common straw one to come from Newcastle and they have not sent it. Also she is in such distress about her poor brother that I feel quite sorry for having had at all to find fault. He does not expect to live many days and she is so hoping that she sees him before he dies. I trust she may, but I fear much that he cannot last till we get to town. I may not write again, and in that case you may expect us on Friday in good time—a large party—Wells, Bella, Heseltine and a man.

[With such a large party it seems incredible that Wells was not released to go straight to London to see her brother. But although Cecilia was sympathetic, it does not seem to have occurred to her to let her go, though on reaching Carlton House Terrace on May 16th she wrote to her mother:]

I feel still in a great hurry and rather bewildered by it, and I am really distressed at having found that poor Wells's brother died on Sunday night, so that if we had come straight here she would have been just in time. Is it not very sad? And those days at Ampthill were so delightful to me. I feel as if I had been very selfish about it, and I hardly like to look at Wells. She is in great grief. She went away before I was up this morning, so Heseltine has been nurse today and a very nice comfortable one.

CHAPTER FOURTEEN

The Twins

THE summer of 1844 was again spent in London and there are no letters to cover the period. They returned to Blagdon on July 21st and Cecilia immediately sat down and wrote to her mother:

We arrived a few hours ago and have just had a comfortable meal of coffee, mutton chops and figs. We met Mr. Dawson just as we were going into Newcastle, so I had an interview with him. I gave him Dr. Ferguson's prescription and he said he perfectly agreed and would make it up for me.

When I arrived here I found the rocking horse, to my surprise, already established upstairs in the passage, so for the present I must leave it there. Little Matt was so excited with it and with all the various little toys he found again that he seemed quite beside himself, and at last had many good fits of crying in consequence. Baby looked very pleased. He has got such a nice colour and looks very well, little pet.

I have been into the flower garden. It is very backward and will not be in beauty for some time, but I think it will look nice when all the flowers are out.

July 1844   *Blagdon*

I have been busy today talking and contriving with Turner how to get more rain water into the laundry, and to get it filtered like that at Ampthill, and I expect we have made a beautiful arrangement, but really it is very difficult to understand all the various pipes and cisterns and stopcocks etc. about the house.

I really do not know what to say, *dearest* Mama, about your coming here so late. You know that I should like, of course, that you should come here directly and stay all the time, and that the greatest possible delight and pleasure to me is to be with you as much as possible. But you are so much more wise and sensible than I am that you will no doubt judge best what is the best to do. How much happier I should be if Matt was always anxious to have you all with us, which I am sure he would be if it were not for *some one*, and *will* be sooner or later. But I suppose one must learn to bear things which are different to one's wishes and consider them as needful discipline for one. It will be delightful to have you all here. Wells is in a beautiful humour.

24 July 1844   *Blagdon*

We have a regular rainy day, having just pitched a tent on the lawn and prepared ourselves for living out of doors. However, I hope it will not last. Yesterday it was very hot and oppressive. The chicks were out all day and I very nearly so. I drew an ash tree, most shockingly, and this morning I find someone has *dusted* it, which does not signify, as it was so bad. I felt as if I had lost the *knack* of doing it. I went to the school in the morning and found it going on pretty well, though the children are not quite so neat as I should like.

I had a note from Lady Elizabeth Grey inviting us to attend the ceremony of laying the first stone of their new church.[1] They have service first at their parish church and then go to the site of the other. I felt a great wish to go, but Matt thought it would be too much for me, and a great crowd with a good deal of standing, so very unwillingly I gave it up. However, I think I shall go to luncheon afterwards. Dr. Hook is to be there to preach.[2] . . . I am expecting Mr. Dawson today. I suppose my confinement will not be before the 27th of September, but really I do feel so enormous now that I do not know what I shall do if I go on increasing all that time. Wee Baby

---

[1] St. James's Church, Morpeth.

[2] Walter Farquhar Hook (1798–1875) was Vicar of Leeds 1837–59. His published works included *A Church Dictionary*, *An Ecclesiastical Biography*, and *Lives of the Archbishops of Canterbury*.

has got his eighth tooth and has begun his shoes and stockings. His feet look like little dolls' feet in them. Wells continues very delightful.

[Cecilia did not have to wait another two months, for three days after the last letter, on 27 July, she gave birth prematurely to boy and girl twins. The girl, Mary, lived to grow up, but the boy survived only three weeks and died on 18 August 1844. It is remarkable that even one of them survived in those days, when so little was known about the care of premature babies. There is no letter telling of their birth, but on 22 August Cecilia wrote to her mother:]

Blagdon

Dearest Mama, I should have written to you some days ago if we had not been so engrossed with misery about our poor little boy, and by this time you will know, of course, that we have lost him, and that his poor little companion, whom we thought so much less likely to do well, is still spared to us and improving gradually every day. I feel very glad that Papa saw the two poor little twins together. The day he was here they were quite well and I was so happy at seeing him that his visit did me a great deal of good and I felt as well as possible after it. . . . I long to talk it all over with you, dearest Mama. When is that to be?

From the first I had quite understood that we could hardly expect them both to do well, and indeed, when I looked at their tiny little thin limbs, it was hardly possible to think they could ever become strong and healthy. And yet, after a time, when I was always told they were doing so well, I had quite begun to look forward to their growing up, and it was very hard to part with my tiny darling. Now I hardly dare to hope that the little girl may do well, she is so very, very weak and delicate. But even if she is taken from us I shall be very thankful to have had a little Mary, even for such a short time. She is still unable to suck, so that the wet nurse was of no use to her and would not stay, but I shall feel much more happy about her as soon as I can have another for her. The two other children are so well and so happy, it is charming to see them, and little Matt is immensely improved. Pray write to me, dearest Mama. I wish you were here.

[To this Lady Parke replied on 25 August, from Gilsland where they were staying with Charles Howard for the grouse-shooting. Considering that she was only forty-five miles from Blagdon, it is extraordinary that she did not go to see Cecilia, but Sir Matthew was opposing it, with the best intentions, in Cecilia's interest.]

My darling Child, I just open my letter to tell you that I have yours and with what joy I have had the comfort of hearing from yourself. Bless you and may a merciful Father comfort you in your trouble. I hope and believe that you are able to bear up, for you will, I am sure, cast your care upon Him who cares for all, and your little darling Mary will be spared if it is right that this should be. I think you are so right to decide upon a wet nurse, for of course she must have one when she can take the breast. I never heard that a wet nurse brings her child until the poor wee can take enough to relieve the breast. Ask Mr. Dawson this, for I really could not recommend anything, and you are so well able to judge yourself about this and all other things.

The Judge is on the moors today, or he would add his fondest love, and you must tell Sir Matthew that I will not plague him with a letter today, but beg you to give him my thanks for his of yesterday. I hope that you may read my letter without the smallest fear of any injury to your dear eyes, and I must also hope that you will be as well after the expiration of your month as it is reasonable to expect. Cheer up, darling. I wish I was with you.

Your very affectionate mother, C. Parke.

25 August 1844   *Blagdon*

Dearest Mama, I must write to you a little today. The sun is shining and I am in hopes I may at last be able to go out for a little while, which will do me more good than anything. The monthly nurse is just gone and the little girl is transferred into the hands of Wells, who is in a state of great excitement, as unfortunately it so happens we have no additional maid yet. The little girl is better today than she has yet been, but she has not yet got a particle of fat and her skin is quite loose, which gives her a look of age that makes one uncomfortable. It is quite impossible to imagine anything so thin and small and skinny as her legs. The poor little boy's face had become quite fat and he had a great likeness to little Matt, but I suppose it was not real healthy fat but a kind of swelling, and it went away quite suddenly when he was taken ill. I feel glad that the little girl is in Wells's hands, for she is so very attentive, and the old nurse was not so much so, and I did not feel quite sure that she was always taking as much care as she ought. She had evidently never been with a lady before and her ways were not very nice; besides she was very noisy in her movements. But she was careful and I think on the whole I was lucky to get so good a one considering the circumstances. My recovery has been very good indeed. There was only one day when I was at all uncomfortable, and I have gone on better than Mr. Dawson expected I could possibly do. I am very thankful that the premature confinement was not brought on by anything that could have been avoided. I should have been so miserable when I saw the two little delicate creatures if I had thought that any imprudence or fatigue had occasioned it all, but Mr. Dawson says it was certainly nothing of the sort, but only the fact of there being *two*. Was it not very fortunate that it did not happen on the road? I am now so well that I think even Matt must very soon be convinced that it can do me no harm to have the excitement of your being here. I do so long for you.

[Evidently Sir Matthew was convinced, for Lord and Lady Parke came to stay at Blagdon on 29 August. The day before they arrived Cecilia wrote to her mother:]

You will, from your experience, expect to find Matt in a fussy state. You would have been quite pleased if you had seen him in all our trouble about the little twins. He was so tender and full of feeling and affection and so distressed and grieved about the poor little boy. I never saw a papa more fond of his children. I think there are very few so patient and nice with them when they are so little. You will think little Matt very much improved, at least I hope so. He is so manly and so happy and I think on the whole a very good child. Wells has been in a very amiable temper and she won my heart just now by being so pleased when I told her you were coming. The little girl is pretty well and she still goes on being fed, and I find that Matt's determination against a wet nurse is increased to a formidable degree. However, he will consent to have one the moment the feeding disagrees, and that is all I can obtain. At present she could not suck, so I hope we are doing the best for her.

September 1844   *Blagdon*

Today I have been all the way to the sea at Cambois, where I walked wondrously, made a very trumpery sketch and found several new flowers. Tomorrow I hope to go to Morpeth. We think of beginning a small tour on Wednesday . . . As we were sitting on the beach by the sea an old man came up and gave Matt a pat with his stick across the shoulders and then sat down with us and talked most familiarly. He tried to make out where we came from, and at last he asked me if I knew who the gentleman was. I said "I believe Sir Matthew Ridley." "Oh no, it can't be," said he; "one of his servants you mean."

[On 19 September they set out for their "small tour," going to Edinburgh by way of Wooler, Kelso and Melrose. Cecilia wrote on 25 September:]

Douglas Hotel, Edinburgh

We are just arrived at Edinburgh and alas, my troubles are come once again, for I find here a letter from Wells telling me that the wet nurse has lost all her milk entirely, and in consequence the little girl is not quite so well. It is very grievous. I have written for another to be sent immediately, but I feel as if there was a fate against my having one to do well, and although it does not seem advisable to go back home directly, yet I should not wonder if tomorrow's account were to make us do so, and at any rate one must feel anxious and uncomfortable . . .

We made a day from Kelso to Melrose, spending some time at Dryburgh Abbey on the way, and this morning we left Melrose and have had a long drive here. The ruins are splendid, but there are too many tourists there and it is too hackneyed. I am all the better for the journey.

29 September 1844   *Edinburgh*

We heard this morning a sermon on the unity of the Church, and the minister seemed to agree in many of his sentiments with Dr. Arnold's. The part of the service which pleased me the most was a christening of three children. It was done in a way which I liked much better than that of our own Church, except that I felt that so much must depend upon the minister, and that one never could be sure of it with a minister one did not know.

All this time I have not told you that I am not comfortable about matters at home, and have half a wish to set off directly and go back. My last account from Wells said that, after all, the nurse would not do, the baby had not been so well, and she had got the old cowman's daughter who lives close by, and as Mr. Dawson had approved of her she was to nurse the little girl, for the present at any rate. I have had since that a letter from Mr. Dawson saying the Baby was much better, and this evening I had a letter from the wet nurse complaining of ill usage on the part of Wells, and saying she had been treated unfairly. It is difficult at this distance to judge, but I daresay Wells has been unkind, and I am really sorry, for it is a serious thing to have to make so many changes. I fear temper has had to do with this.

This is a very noisy inn. They are mincing beef in the kitchen below, a bell rings every two or three minutes just outside, and there is such a running about and talking, it is quite awful. We mean to leave on Wednesday and to go by Dunbar, Berwick, Bamburgh, etc. to the Bryan Burrells' at Bolton near Alnwick. We are to go to Alnwick for the Sessions.

5 October 1844   *Blagdon*

Dearest Mama, At last I can sit down to write to you a comfortable letter, and really I have been quite distressed at not writing to you

for so many days, but it has been really impossible—for what with my
company and my nursery and my business of various kinds, every
instant has been occupied. Everybody is just gone, and now we are
alone. I must tell you, to begin with, that I am very cross and bothered
and annoyed, though quite well, so my humour must account for any
unpleasant tone in my letter and you must make allowances for it.
In the first place I find the children so changed that I am quite
annoyed. Little Matt has got back all his fretty, crying ways and does
nothing but scream and cry. He does not look happy, and in short he
is quite different, and little Edward cries much more than he did, so
that I really think Wells has mismanaged them very much, and it is
really a serious thing, for it ruins the dispositions of the little pets. I
was so happy to think little Matt so improved and so nice, and now
the change is quite striking. I hope it will go off again, but it is
provoking, particularly as we had people here to see it, and I know
Mrs. John Cookson will tell everybody and make the worst of it.
Wells gave me a long history about the wet nurse and made out that
she had lost all her milk, and that she behaved ill in going away without saying a word to anybody, and Mr. Dawson tells me that it was
entirely owing to her temper, and he says that the nurse told him she
was constantly worried and tormented, so that she could not really
stay. He advised me to give up the baby entirely to the wet nurse,
but I think it would not answer to do that, and I must try and watch
and prevent the poor woman being annoyed. We have one now who
seems very nice and respectable and quiet, and I really hope she will
stay, though I begin to despair of it. In the midst of all this I am
sorry to say that Wells has got a fit of the grumps again.

Sunday, 6 October 1844   *Blagdon*

I think you will be anxious about my state of mind, and I am happy
to say that it is many degrees better today, and that I feel as if I was
emerging from a fit of black dog. The children are getting back to
their happy state by degrees, Wells has ceased to be under the
dominion of the grumps, the John Cooksons are gone, Baby is better,
and altogether things in general are improved. I find little Matt
much come on in talking and intelligence, though much more difficult

to manage. He has been out all day and always with only a nursery-maid, and Wells has been too engrossed by the *wee* to pay much attention to managing him. When she is anxious she is so fussy that she makes a more than needful business of it all. I wish we had not had people here just when we came back, for I know they will carry away a bad impression. However, perhaps it is good for one's vanity, and one cannot have everything just as one wishes.

CHAPTER FIFTEEN

Autumn 1844

October 1844   *Blagdon*

Charles Ridley has been here. His leave was out and he was
obliged to go yesterday. I do not like him. He is agreeable and was
very kind to me and very affectionate, but I do not think he has right
feelings about things, he seems so very bitter and violent, and I really
felt quite afraid of him. He does not appear to have a speck of love
for his mother left, and though one cannot wonder at it, yet I did not
like to hear him at every opportunity giving her a violent *hit*. He
spoke once of the state of affairs and said that Matt ought to have
remonstrated with her more decidedly, and that the only way to
manage her was to drive her quite *frantic*. I said I could not imagine
anyone treating a mother in such a way. He has left altogether a
painful impression with me, and though I am very glad he has been
I am equally glad he is gone.

We went to pay our bridal visit to Mrs. Oswin Cresswell and I was
very much pleased with her.[1] She is a ladylike looking person and
very frank and pleasing in her manner and seems likely to be a great
acquisition in the neighbourhood. She is very communicative about
herself and told me immediately that she was in that situation in
which it was thought bad for her to drive over rough roads. She also
told me all about her having been ill, owing to walking too much,
which had brought on a *mishap* some months ago. She had a little
sister of seven years old with her and seems very happy, and really

[1] Anne Seymour, eldest daughter of Sir William Gordon Cumming,
married in 1843 Oswin Cresswell, eldest son of Baker Cresswell of Cresswell Hall, Northumberland. Her younger sister married his brother
William Cresswell in 1852.

there is something prepossessing about her. She has so much character and is so naive and lively. She is a very picturesque looking person and has a great deal of original taste in her arrangement of *herself*. She seems to know a great deal about painting. Mrs. John Cookson does not appear to advantage by her. She has only half the character of Wordsworth's *Skylark*, which he says is "True to the kindred points of Heaven and Home." She is true to *home* but has no thoughts for anything else. She is quite of the earth earthy—a person to whom all little things appear great. However, she is a very devoted, good mother. She had a snub the other night from Matt which I hope nobody heard but me. She began to talk to him of the Colbornes and he stopped her and said she ought to know better than to mention them to him—all of which was very unpleasant and made me so uncomfortable that I could not find a word to say all the evening, so you may imagine the party was not lively. Indeed, during these last days I have felt so stupid and so preoccupied that I could not make the party go off well and it has been fearfully dull. Mrs. Bell is coming to us for one night on Tuesday, and I hope I shall be in a better humour then. I have had a great deal of trouble too about my dress for Alnwick, there is so little time. But Heseltine is a good creature and will do her best to make me tidy.

The garden still keeps up a little show and the dahlias are not killed. The hamper you got contained the Howick geraniums and one or two of our best carnations, besides a few odds and ends. I did not send the white fuchsia because your gardener said he had it. You are a dear good Mama to send me such nice useful accounts of the Woburn beds. I shall study them and try and improve my ways by them. The gowns too were very welcome.

I must finish my lamentations now. It has done me good to pour them out to you and I hope they will not annoy you.

8 October 1844   *Blagdon*

Today I have been with Lady Elizabeth Grey. I went there early and had luncheon and then we drove together to Mitford and found Mrs. Mitford out, so we came back and went to see the model of the new church. I think it will be very handsome yet very plain, and I

WILLIAM
DAWSON, M.D.

SARAH
COOKSON

thought the interior promised to be particularly good. Lady Elizabeth showed me a very beautiful letter from Lord Fitzwilliam to Lord Burlington with which I was much struck.[1] It was very short, telling him that he did not wish him to endeavour to avoid the recollection of his loss, but rather advised him to dwell constantly on it. I think people in general are so wrong in giving contrary advice, not only because it is so far less soothing to one's feelings, but also I think it is not the way in which we are intended to receive our sorrows. It is true that a Christian should not give way to grief so as to unfit him for his duties, should not sorrow as those who have no hope, but our consolation should not proceed from turning our thoughts elsewhere.

17 October 1844 *Blagdon*

I must write to you before setting off on our Alnwick jaunt. This is a day of days—quite lovely, so bright and fresh. We have been introducing little Matt to three white rabbits the Burrells sent him and he is extremely delighted. We had an affair of honour this morning, for he refused to put away his things and I told him that if when I came back from the nursery they were not put away he should not go down to breakfast. He did not mind, so I had to send him upstairs amidst great lamentations, which is about the first *punishment* he has had. I find him a very agreeable companion and I like taking him out to walk without any of those odious nurses. Wells is quite in a good humour now, though not remarkably pleasant. I certainly could imagine a more *congenial* nurse, but yet I cannot quite decide to send her away.

I think you managed beautifully about your party. I assure you mine was quite fearfully dull. I do not think I ever recollect anything so *longwhiley*, and I wish I had not taken a dislike to Mrs. Cookson. She was out of her own set and appeared to great disadvantage, and really I could not take to Charles Ridley, much as I was disposed to do so. William is the one I like.

I expect to be very presentable at Alnwick.

[1] Lord Burlington married in 1829 Lady Blanche Howard, sister of Lady Elizabeth Grey and Charles Howard. She died in 1840.

C.R.—M

October 1844   *Blagdon*

We came back from Alnwick this morning, where I enjoyed myself extremely, though I do not like the Duchess so well as before. She is such a thorough *Tory* in Dr. Arnold's sense of the word. She is agreeable certainly, but very narrow minded. She would have been very different if she had had children to make her keep pace with the times. I find people do think her very uncertain and she certainly can look formidable. Yesterday we were out all day, driving in the morning, and afterwards having a long walk with her Grace, who goes railroad pace in spite of having an aversion to them. She took me a long walk but I was not tired at all. The morning before was rather awful—we all sat stitching from ten to one, and very scanty conversation going on, except when her Grace was called out, and then Lady Prudhoe and I had some little talk together. I was rather amused at the conversation with the Duchess. We began about books and I asked her if she had read Dr. Arnold, upon which she began to abuse his *principles*, which made my blood boil. Then someone asked me if I had read *Ellen Middleton*[1] and the Duchess immediately began to inveigh against that *wicked* book. Afterwards, seeing her working a carpet, I unluckily told her about Lady Elizabeth Grey's church carpet, when she exclaimed with great horror how much she disapproved of such things.

It is a formal house. Lord and Lady Prudhoe are both of them very agreeable. She is a dear little thing but looks very delicate and is much distressed at not having any prospect of a child. She has been away to the German Baths and is better for it, but is very delicate still.[2] I begged her to come to us and she said she would some day, but I fear not this winter. She invited us to Stanwick and I should much like to go.

Miss Liddell was there alone, for both Lord and Lady Ravensworth are too ill—indeed I fear they are failing. Lord Ossulston also, sing-

[1] A romance by Lady Georgina Fullerton. She published many novels of which *Ellen Middleton* was the first. It is a stirring melodrama which makes very good reading still.

[2] Lady Prudhoe never had any children, but in spite of her delicacy she lived to the age of ninety-six.

ing beautifully, and both he and Miss Liddell are so lively they did
away with the formality in some degree, singing duets together and
practising polka. By the bye, I must not forget that the said Lord O.
won my heart by the way he spoke of Papa. He seemed to enter so
into his character and wished so much to meet him again. I think he
is an amiable person and pleasing—in spite of all faults. There were
also the Henry Liddells.[1] Miss Henry Liddell is a nice girl and much
improved in looks, but both her papa and brother are very conceited.
There was an old Sir George Rich[2] there who was a *sanglier du
second ordre*.[3] The Duke monopolises the *premier ordre*, or rather
divides it with Sir Charles Monck. Lady Mary Monck is dull, but
so kind and good natured that one cannot help liking her. She was
very affectionate to me and I was sorry she went away yesterday.

On Wednesday we played a game of Commerce which was inter-
minable. Yesterday we worked all the morning and afterwards had
a walk in the rain. The High Sheriff and his lady, Mr. and Mrs.
Collingwood,[4] arrived to dinner and we all went in huge coaches by
torchlight to the ball, which was a very gay and agreeable one—
plenty of people and plenty of light and I saw all my friends and was
quite happy. The park is very fine and of enormous extent, but a
little too full of *art*—false waterfalls and false rocks—and the whole
too trimly kept. This morning both Duke and Duchess were ill, but
I saw her for a moment and she was very kind. I have a great respect
for her but I find the impression she made this time upon me very
different from what it was three years ago, and I suppose I am changed
myself. I think Charles and Dr. Arnold have both had something to
do with it. The Duchess taught me a new little poddling way of

[1] Henry Liddell succeeded his father as the second Lord Ravensworth in 1855 and was created first Earl of Ravensworth in 1874. He
married in 1820 Isabella Horatia, eldest daughter of Lord George
Seymour.

[2] Sir George Rich (1786–1858) was Chamberlain to the household of
the vice-regal court of Ireland during the government of the Marquess
of Wellesley (1821–28).

[3] *Sanglier* = boar = bore.

[4] Edward John Collingwood (1815–95), of Chirton and Lilburn,
married in 1842 Anna, second daughter of Arthur Burdett.

knitting, to make little round mats like starfishes, which she works at all the evening as if she were a distressed gentlewoman.

October 1844   *Blagdon*

I was the whole day yesterday at Newcastle and came back as hoarse as a raven. However, this morning my voice is restored to its usual sound and I am particularly well. I was occupied chiefly in buying for my club, for which I shall have nearly £50 to spend this year. Some of the people have begged to give a £ a pair for blankets. Is that not grand? I had a great many things to do but did not find time for half. I paid a visit to young Richardson and settled to begin having lessons after next week, but I will be obliged to go to him because he will not come to me. He had some pretty sketches in his room and was beginning a large picture of Derwentwater which promised well. He will very likely be of use to me, though I should doubt that he understood teaching particularly well.

I must tell you now about the chicks. Little weeny is growing visibly and really looks now like a wee little baby about a week old. The nurse is very nice, such a steady, pleasing woman with a manner that I should like to transplant into Wells very much. They seem to get on beautifully together and I have heard no fault found yet, so I really hope this time it may do well. Mr. Dawson desired me to let the baby sleep with the nurse, which I do.

Alas, all my dahlias died last Saturday except about three, and everything else was so blown about that I must give up looking at the garden except the little bits under the windows which are still gay.

October 1844   *Blagdon*

I meant to write to you yesterday, but the day went by without my doing it, so today I shall take a *large* sheet and begin in good earnest. I am sorry to say that I am just now sitting in the nursery and feeling rather uneasy about poor little Edward. Mr. Dawson was here yesterday and said there was no chance of measles and that he would not come back till Thursday. But today he seems so very unwell that I have just dispatched a note to beg Mr. D. to come this afternoon. The little darling is languid and heavy and seems as if his head was affected, which makes me uneasy. Yesterday it was his chest but now that appears relieved. I will tell you what the doctor says afterwards. Little Matt is very well and has been out today. He is in great spirits and delights in going to the kitchen with me to see "Miss Du" as he calls Mrs. Drury. He inherits some of his Papa's taste, for yesterday I appeared in that old favourite gown with a red stripe, and he ran up to me directly, saying "Oh *pity* gown." The small sister is doing beautifully. Heseltine had not seen her since you were here, two months ago, for she does not visit Wells, so she took the opportunity of seeing her when she was in her solitary room and she was quite delighted with the improvement.

The Blands[1] come tomorrow, and today Riddells, Selbys, etc. It is unfortunate altogether, for if dear little Edward is not much better I shall not be able to enjoy having them, nor to go with them to the ball tomorrow. I have been busy this morning arranging flowers, and making comfortable *corners*, and trying to teach Bevan how to put books and chairs with an unformal look.

I must tell you that I gave Wells such a lecture the other day. I am quite amazed at myself when I think of it. I told her such unpleasant truths. I really had something of Ellen Middleton's feelings when she poured out all her wrongs, and I felt all the time astonished at my own courage. It was all caused by her complaining so of having the baby taken from her, which was so ridiculous. She seemed much inclined not to receive the nurse back very kindly, so that I told her that if she did not go on quite well with her I should put the baby entirely under her care, for I did not mean to part with this nurse.

Did I tell you that I saw Mrs. Coulson on my way from Alnwick? She had not seen anyone, but Lady Byron took me in for a minute. She looked very thin and weak, but she is quite better and I hope she is soon going into the south for the winter. Lord and Lady Byron came down not expecting to find her alive. Mr. Dawson says the attack was brought on by degrees—by the great exposure to cold she had always liked. She thought it did her good, but she must not do so again. That reminds me of myself and my hoarseness. It is quite

---

[1] The Blands of Kippax Park, Yorkshire. Their daughter Mary married Charles Weld. Apollonia never married.

gone and Mr. D. has given me a nice bracing gargle which does me good.

Later. Mr. Dawson has been and says it is nothing to make one at all uneasy. He says it is a little nervous irritation from the eye teeth.

October 1844   *Blagdon*

I must snatch a minute to write to you this morning. The Blands came yesterday and went to the ball and seemed to enjoy it much. They danced constantly and looked very nice. Mrs. Bland is not well and could not dine downstairs, but she is better today. We went fourteen to the ball—four young ladies and five young gentlemen. I was very tired indeed and delighted to come away and it was not a very good ball. I was not up to dancing at all. I felt rather uncomfortable at leaving my little man, but he is a little better today, though still uneasy with those nasty teeth. Mr. Dawson says there is nothing to make one anxious. It is all I can do to make Wells give the medicine he orders. Little Matt was down yesterday but made himself so disagreeable that I rather dread taking him today. It is very tiresome of him and I do not know what to do to him. Some of our party are gone and others are coming. Mrs. Charles Bigge[1] is very musical so we can have some singing tonight and perhaps a round game if the time allows it. Mr. Ord[2] has been here and left this morning. He is lively and *useful* but rather forward I think.

2 November 1844   *Blagdon*

Yesterday Little Matt had become familiar with company and had lost all fears, and the Blands were very kind to him, and he was even satisfied to stay with them without me, which I thought very wonderful. Poor little Edward was obliged to receive his company upstairs and he always looked as pleasant as possible to see anyone. Mrs. Bland was very kind and I felt so sorry to part so soon from her. I should have liked a day or two alone with her. She is not at all strong

[1] Charles Bigge, of Linden near Morpeth, married in 1802 Alicia, only daughter of Christopher Wilkinson of Newcastle-upon-Tyne.

[2] William Ord, barrister and M.P. for Newport, Isle of Wight. He married the daughter of William Loraine of Kirkharle.

but she dined twice with us and looked extremely nice. We had no round games, for the music proved very engrossing and they were all delighted with Mrs. Bigge's singing. Apollonia and Mary did not get on quite so well, for they had bad colds and Mary's voice was rather the worse for hers. She is a nice, frank, merry girl and is looking handsome, but Apollonia I thought seemed very *puny* and spiritless.

I have just got your letter, which is quite a *treat*. I should not like so *shapely* a cloak but I like the idea of chinchilly. I have a cerise silk, very rich, which I am thinking of making up and trimming with my handsome lace. Do you think it would do? I am inclined to think it would and then I should not want another.

4 November 1844   *Blagdon*

I have had my drawing lesson today at Newcastle—two hours from Mr. Richardson. I am a little disappointed with him, for I thought him slightly poddling. He took a sketch of mine and began a coloured drawing from it, and he kept saying all the time that he could not get the shape of the woods so nice as mine, which did not sound *Masterlike*. I am afraid he will not do me much good, but perhaps I ought not to judge the first time. It was a most unpleasant day—east wind and rain by turns. I had to order a bird cage for four canaries, and I had also to see about making up a piece of work of Mrs. John Cookson's for a screen. I found it would cost £5, which I grudge extremely, for it is not pretty, the subject being *a black man's head*. Is it not embarrassing to know what to do, for I wish to do it honour to please her, and yet it is so very sad to give so much for it.

I think you are quite right in all you say about my parting with Wells, but I really believe it has been very good for me to have her and has given me a slight degree of *decision* which I had not before. However, I think I have had education sufficient from her now.

11 November 1844   *Blagdon*

We have had a sad business here lately—the chief pump in the house had acquired a dreadful smell which I was convinced was making the place unhealthy. So I spoke to Turner and insisted upon having the well opened out and thoroughly cleaned. He had it done immediately, and the man who went down (one of our own masons) staid three hours at the bottom and was seized directly afterwards with violent cramp and inflammation which has nearly cost him his life. I hope he is better now but it is a sad affair.

Tomorrow the house will be quite full of Shelleys[1] and others. Today we have only the Bryan Burrells, for I wished to have Mrs. B. one day alone as I really like her. Charles will be here on Monday and I have asked the Greys to come over on Thursday. I am only sorry we have people—Mrs. Mitford and the Bells, and the old Cooksons. I do not like to have the Greys then, for old Mr. Cookson abuses them dreadfully. I hope he will not do it before Charles. I shall not be able to go to Morpeth before, as I shall be engaged with my company. I am also slightly afraid of an open carriage just now, for I have a tiresome cough which Mr. Dawson says is of no consequence, but as it has lasted some time I mean to send it away as quick as I can. Will you tell me, dearest Mama, whether you think a brooch of Scotch pebbles would do as a wedding present for Lizzy Sinclair?

November 1844   *Blagdon*

Hark, Hark, the dogs do bark! The Johnstones are coming—whether they be in jags or rags or velvet gowns I cannot say, not having yet seen the light of their countenances.[2] Egerton Harcourt will be here at dinner too.

I am afraid you have had a great deal of trouble about cloaks. I daresay the one you saw will be very nice, and could I not have it either with Ampthill lace or a nice fringe? for I really cannot afford the 24 £s, and indeed I think it would be foolish to have so handsome a lace for constant winter wear. I have a good deal to ask your advice about. First—Heseltine with all trying cannot cut the waist and sleeves without another half yard of velvet, there is so small a piece

[1] Sir John Shelley, sixth Baronet, of Maresfield Park, Tunbridge Wells, married Frances, only daughter and heiress of Thomas Wrinckley of Brookholes, Lancashire.

[2] Sir John Johnstone, second Baronet, of Hackness Hall, Yorkshire, married in 1825 Louisa, second daughter of Edward Harcourt, Archbishop of York. They had two sons and four daughters.

left from my evening waist. Shall I have the half yard more or make up the black satin? The velvet is enough to make a waist and *one sleeve*—can I go with one arm sleeveless? Second—What shall I do for my black net evening gown? Should it have folds for the waist? And if so, should they not be of stiff black net, or do you think a bertha done round with twiddled up ribbon? I think folds would perhaps be best, then I shall want the twiddled ribbons for flounces. Thirteen yards and the bertha would take more—about four yards.

I have got a bad cold and have been obliged to resort to *pridolette.*

November 1844   *Blagdon*

Lady Johnstone is very pleasant and the girls look very nice. They don't dine or breakfast in company. Last night we had a little dancing and *Chasse le Lièvre* and I had a great deal of fun with Egerton. Lady Elizabeth is always the same and it would have been delightful if they could have staid longer, I should have enjoyed having them all to myself. Mrs. Mitford looks bitter and cross, poor thing. Mrs. Bell was nice and conversational and the Cadogans did very well. Little Matt was sometimes quite sensible and sometimes as shy as possible, but he is quite at his ease with Charles and evidently must recollect him. He insists upon it that the black man in the worked screen is *Grandpapa.* He and little Eddy are both in plaid frocks and really look very nice. I did not mean Eddy to begin, but he looked so starved by the side of his brother that I thought they had better be alike. I am really ashamed now of saying that I *have made up my mind*, but I really think I have, not to keep Wells much longer, so I should be very grateful if you will be on the look out. I think I shall give her warning on the first fair opportunity.

Charles and I have had some nice reading together and we think *Vigilantius* very interesting.[1] He seems very well.

December 1844   *Blagdon*

We have a better day at last and it looks really go-outable, which it has not lately. I have a great deal to say at the school and must go

---

[1] *Vigilantius and His Times*, by W. S. Gilly, 1844.

there, for Christmas is a great epoch there, and there are to be prizes and examinations and all sorts of things. I think I must give a lecture on tidiness, for the mistress is not particular enough and does not set the best example in that respect. Yesterday was very damp and disagreeable, but I went to church and had a little *run* afterwards to warm myself.

Charles Ridley told us in his letter that Miss Harriet Browne was to have £25,000 at her mother's death, so that they will be well off then. At present they do not know what Lord Oranmore can give her, for his affairs are in very great disorder. I had a *beautiful* note from her yesterday which I must show you one day. It has quite made me *take to her*.

I do not think myself looking the *least* beautiful—on the contrary rather *raggy*, but I am much better today and my cough is nearly gone—indeed it is nothing now.

CHAPTER SIXTEEN

Illness

ALTHOUGH Cecilia made light of her cough and did not complain at all seriously about her health, she was iller than she admitted to her mother, or even to herself. It is clear from the description of her symptoms in the ensuing letters that she had contracted tuberculosis, possibly from the butler, Bateman. It was never recognised by Mr. Dawson or Sir John Fife, but their means of diagnosis were very limited and her condition was complicated by the fact that she had stopped menstruating. This often happens in advanced stages of tuberculosis, but the possibility of her being pregnant obscured the diagnosis. Sir Matthew, however, was obviously anxious about her, for he recorded in his diary, which was usually concerned entirely with estate matters and quite impersonal, that on 17 December, while they were visiting the John Cooksons at Benwell, she felt "some weakness and debility. She continued to go to church, however," he added, "until Christmas Day." On 23 December Cecilia wrote:

Blagdon

We are very quiet here at present, entirely alone, with the exception of an unfortunate painter who is making portraits of horses and lives with the servants, only occasionally emerging into the upper regions. William Ridley is coming this week, but otherwise we expect no one, and I mean to employ myself in making myself quite strong, for I have not been feeling very well lately. My little people are all well and daily becoming more understanding. Little Matt often talks about Grandpapa and Grandmama. He was taken today to see the geese in the larder, which seemed to strike him very much.

24 December 1844   *Blagdon*

How very good *Punch's Almanack*[1] is. We have been laughing over it this evening—we meaning William and I, for Matt has been so sound asleep that his little parcel from you has had no chance yet. Today a large heifer has been divided amongst 270 people, who will all have good dinners tomorrow. Little Matt was immensely struck with the great joints of meat, which he called "arge chops" and "arge pings." He is great fun sometimes and talks more every day, and little Edward is regaining his roses but still looks thin. Baby's face is really almost as big as his now, she is so very fat and firm and nice with it. I am sorry to say that Bella is going away, concerning which there is a history as follows: Wells told me she had heard her say to little Matt one day he must lie down or the man would fetch him, and other things of that kind, which I told her I considered so wrong that if she continued to frighten him so I could not keep her. So after this, it seems, she went to Bella, told her she would turn her out of the house without a character, and abused her so altogether that the poor girl said she could not stay any longer. She acknowledged she had said the things and was very sorry, but she said that though her place was comfortable, yet at times it was hardly possible to endure Wells. I am sorry she is going, for she is a good, steady girl and it is not very easy to find just what one wants.

Christmas Day 1844   *Blagdon*

I have received your dear little Christmas box, and thank you very much for it. It is so pretty and useful and I think it is so nice to have a Christmas box—I am quite pleased with it.

I believe all you say in the medical line is true, and I am sure Mr. Dawson began giving me tonics the other day when I was not fit for them. He is now, he says, *preparing* me for quinine. It is difficult to say what is the matter with me, for it is only that I am not strong and have rather a dislike to all food. I feel as if I was becoming very fanciful about myself, but I hope I shall get over that soon. One thing that weakens me is that I have such excessive perspirations at night, but Mr. D. thinks nothing of that, or of any of my ailments,

[1] *Punch* was founded in 1841.

and says I am soon to mount my pony and ride about and be as well as possible.

We have been reading *The Chimes*[1] and I am in the middle of Trotty's dream and wishing he would wake to get rid of it. I am disappointed in it hitherto and I think the Goblins talk a lot of nonsense.

I have seen nothing of the Greys, to my great sorrow. They have no horses and Mr. Dawson told me I had better not go out at present. I went, however, well wrapt to church today and am no worse at all.

People have not admired little Edward lately, so that I think he must be less pretty, though I do not perceive it. Lady Shelley was quite rude about him. He is a dear little engaging thing and looks such a thorough well bred little gentleman, but he does not grow much.

2 January 1845   *Blagdon*

Dearest Alice, Little Matt has been in a great state of excitement today about some toys that Mr. Dawson brought yesterday as a New Year's gift. His state of delight is not to be conceived, particularly with those given to *Edward*. . . . I have deserted my drawing altogether for a while. However, I soon mean to begin again and go on vigorously if possible. I play the harp every evening regularly, though sometimes only for ten minutes, but that I consider very virtuous and I hope you will think so too.

4 January 1845   *Blagdon*

Dearest Mama, I am still going on improving and am gradually regaining my own appetite, which you know to be a very good one. Mr. Dawson says there is a *very* great and decided change and I expect to be able to go to Woolsington next week if I continue to feel better. We have been engaged to that visit for a long time. I do not expect to like it, and I was half in hopes secretly that Mr. D. would say I had better not go. But he did not, so of course I shall go if possible. My cough is very much less frequent and so are my nightly

[1] *The Chimes* was Dickens's second Christmas book, published in 1844, and not so popular as *A Christmas Carol* (1843).

discomforts, which are now about every third or fourth night instead of every night.

My little Matt is rather on the invalid list today, but I hope it will be nothing, and little Eddy fell on his nose yesterday and was obliged to have a little dose administered to him. The baby is beginning to be quite interesting—she laughs and coos and looks as pleasant as possible. She comes down every day and has a walk up and down the room, and then I take her for a little whilst the nurse plays with the other children and she lies on my lap smiling and as good as possible. Sometimes Wells chooses to bring her down instead of nurse, which is a disagreeable change, though she is very humble and sweet at present. I often see *black looks* and think now my opportunity is coming, but they always blow over and I believe I shall have to wait until just before we go to town, when I must tell her she is not to return.

I have begun Arnold's *Rome*[1] and cannot at present find any good map, which is a bore. However, I think there is one somewhere, if not I must buy one. I have finished *The Monastery* and do not admire it, and now I am deep in *The Abbot* which appears to me very superior. I hope to have the *Edinburgh Review* today—is there any Macaulay in it?

Monday January 1845   *Blagdon*

I must write you a few lines to tell you the result of Sir John Fife. He seemed perfectly to agree with Mr. Dawson in all his views, but they have made a change in my diet and in the medicine. I am to eat no meat and drink no wine, but take broth, arrowroot pudding etc., and soda water as much as I can. I am not to go out just now, and to keep myself very warm. I have had two bad nights and rather feverish, but they say they can put a stop to that directly and that I am to sleep like a top tonight. They again examined my lungs and said they were quite remarkably healthy. Sir J. Fife says a few days will see a great change in me. I am glad to have had him, as it makes one feel more comfortable. He was astonished at the baby and said she was disfigured with fat, but that she was a very pretty child.

[1] *History of Rome*, by Thomas Arnold (3 vols., 1838–43).

Wednesday, January 1845 *Blagdon*

I have had a busy day today. First came Mrs. Bell, then the doctors and lastly Lady Stanley.[1] I am decidedly much better and I think my new diet and medicine will suit me. I have had two very much better nights with a gentle perspiration all through instead of a violent one coming on towards morning. My cough too is *much* less frequent and less painful, and my chest now does not feel sore at all. In short I really am wonderfully improved and though I am taking no tonic or wine I feel stronger. I have been breakfasting on arrow-root, but am now going to begin boiled bread and milk and they say I must breakfast upstairs. I have chicken broth, pudding and soda water for luncheon and the same for dinner, jelly at about five, generally, and arrowroot again at ten. But now they say I may eat a *wee* bit of meat if I like. I am not to talk much, which is unlucky.

I am very much interested in Arnold and read it a great deal, but I am beginning to find my eyes weak and am obliged to take care of them by candlelight. I got through dinner very well and feel really quite strong. Lady Stanley talks away and is very kind. Mr. Myers is dead.

Thursday, January 1845 *Blagdon*

The doctors were both here again this morning and made no change, except that I am to have assafoetida, which from its name must be dreadful, and indeed I once did smell it, which was quite enough. . . . My cough began about the beginning of September. I think the huskiness you noticed when you were at Blagdon was the beginning of it.

February 1845. PRIVATE REALLY *Blagdon*

Dearest Mama, I meant to write you such a long letter today, but after all it must be a note. I have had a tiring day—first of all by the much too great effects of a small pill I took last night. Then Mr. D. came and tired me by again trying his stethoscope on every possible

[1] Sir Thomas Stanley, ninth Baronet, of Hooton, Cheshire, married in 1805 Mary, only daughter of Sir Carnaby Haggerston, Bart., of Haggerston Castle, Northumberland.

spot of my chest and back, afterwards telling me for about the hundredth time that my lungs were perfect. In spite of the discomfort I felt today, he declared it was the best day I had had. He said there was a great change in the expectoration for the better and that I should now lose all cough entirely. They have faint ideas of sending me away when I am in a fit state, but nothing more. Mr. D. once said to the west coast, but they will talk it over together and decide what is best when the time comes.

I have got a black silk for morning in Newcastle and a sort of *barège* for evening, which I shall make very warm by lining with silk and long sleeves, but I want a shawl to wear in the house and to be warm and nice looking. Do you think you could pick up one somewhere? I would trust quite to your taste, only I do not want one all black. I fancy there are soft woollen and silk that would do.

I do not much care for a novel. I delight in Dr. Arnold, only the book is so heavy to hold that it tires me. Otherwise I really wish for nothing better. I save my eyes a good deal in the evening.

You cannot think how unnatural I am. Do you know that it bores me to have the children with me? Is it not shocking of me.

Goodbye, dearest Mama. Your very affectionate daughter, C. R.

February 1845   *Blagdon*

The package arrived this evening and I like the shawl much. I think it promises to make itself useful. The books I am sure to like —they are just in my way—you could not have sent anything more so. I am going on well and gaining strength, only slightly troubled today and yesterday by the assafoetida, which refuses to have any effect on me. The weather is dreadful today—a piercing wind and snow all the afternoon. I, however, am very snug in my little corner and feel nothing of it. It is reported with truth that the living of Stannington is given to Mr. Collinson of Gateshead. It sounds well, except that he already has nine children. I should think him likely to be a very good sort of man but I know nothing of him.[1]

[1] Mr. Collinson did not prove to be such a good sort of man as Cecilia hoped. Although he remained at Stannington until his death in 1870, Mary, writing to Lady Parke (or Lady Wensleydale as she then was),

February 1845   *Blagdon*

I feel so much better today that I must write to you. The doctors were here this morning, and Sir John Fife thought so well of me that he is not coming for four days. They have made out a new plan for me—first I am to have a plaister on my chest (I cannot tell why). Then I am twice a day to have some very horrible medicine to affect the expectoration, my sleeping draught at half past six, and a pill at night. I am to have *café au lait* before I get up, boiled milk and bread for breakfast, a good luncheon with one glass of hock, tea at five, and nothing at dinner but a little pudding. I am really going on beautifully.

February 1845   *Blagdon*

I was really tired last night so I begged Matt to write to you. Mrs. J. Cookson had been here, then the doctors twain who staid long. I believe you are quite right about diet. I shall abstain from fritters, but they tell me marrow bones are particularly light and digestible food. Soda water is what I most delight in, but I haven't yet had courage to try it with milk. I cannot take any wine now.

The shawls are beautiful, only too delicate for this dirty place. If I had anybody with me they would be exactly the thing, but my doctors will not hear of that, and do not even like me to see anyone. They say any talking irritates the chest and quickens my pulses, and Sir John Fife, particularly, makes a great point of it. The cap is *lovely*. I am rather a figure now, for I have on in a morning three or four great shawls, and I cannot think of putting that lovely grey one in companionship with all the grubby old concerns. However, I am going to have a new gown and then I *will be smart*.

I cannot think why you suppose I am soon to be in the south. I never hinted it, for I did not suppose from what Mr. Dawson said that they had any idea of it. I must ask them soon what they *do* think about it. I would rather you sent nothing by George Ridley. We never ask him to the house, so it would not be nice to make use of him.

---

said he was "a disgrace to his high calling." He was much addicted to the bottle, and he and Mr. Carrick were often found drunk together in the fields, after being out all night.

C.R.—N

Little Matt has a large red mark on his leg which has broke. They say it is the frost which has caught it.[1]

February 1845   *Blagdon*

Dearest Alice, A great event has happened since I last wrote to you. I am actually encased in flannel next to the skin, can you believe it? The doctor advised me to do it and said it was to be down to the wrists and ankles and up to the throat. However, I declined the universal application of it, so I have got a wonderful looking sort of nondescript thing all in one, ending below my knees, and really, strange to say, I am extremely comfortable with it and quite rejoice at having been told to wear it. I delight in Lord Malmesbury.[2] I never read a book of the kind I liked so well. Matt is just now reading a novel of James to me, *Agincourt*, and it amuses me more than his usually do.[3]

February 1845   *Blagdon*

Dearest Mama, I hope you were not disappointed at not having a letter from me yesterday. I really do not know why I did not write. I feel *very* much better and more like myself and can walk about with more strength. My cough is now nothing, so very loose that it often does not amount to a cough. I think the fiery stuff has done good and it does not hurt now, after having been so often put on. I have had a slight bother, for yesterday Nurse told me that Wells was again using her so ill that she could not bear it. So I wrote a note to Wells and told her that she must either behave with uniform kindness to her or give up the baby entirely to her. This morning she spoke to Matt to justify herself and to say how ill Nurse behaved (for I said in my note that I could not speak to her now) so he is going to pacify them as well as he can.

[1] This large red mark sounds much more likely to be erythema nodosum, an allergic skin reaction to a primary tuberculosis infection.

[2] The first Lord Malmesbury's Diaries and correspondence edited by his grandson, the third Lord Malmesbury, and published 1844.

[3] G. P. R. James wrote many historical novels. *Agincourt* was published in 1844. The style of these romances was parodied by Thackeray in *Novels by Eminent Hands*.

Today they say was like spring, so warm and mild, and I could fancy the birds were beginning to sing. My violets are frost bitten but I had a wee bunch today and plenty of lilies of the valley. They are so sweet and always make me think of you. You would grieve for poor Mr. Sydney Smith. How difficult it is to believe that he is gone.[1]

29 February 1845 *Blagdon*

I am actually writing in the afternoon, which is a proof of my being very much better, which indeed I am. This is my third comfortable day and I am beginning to eat a little. Yesterday I had the apple pudding, and it is the first thing I have liked for a very long time. I remain in bed till half past ten (with my books now) and have my breakfast in the middle of dressing, so that I do not begin the day in my sitting room till twelve, and I feel sure it is a good plan. I feel still the inconvenience of not being able to talk much, and there are many little fault-findings which I put off on that account. Wells evidently thinks herself a fixture, but though she is very placid before me, she does tiresome things. Only think of her beginning to give Edward hasty pudding! i.e. oatmeal porridge, for breakfast and by advice of the nurse! He has thriven well upon it I think, and it is *the* great thing that most children here live upon. He has a chop every other day, and a pudding the other. I do not have both the children together now, at least very seldom, and indeed I have had them very little lately. I could only lie still, so it was dull for them, and the least noise annoyed me and made me feel cross. (Do you know that feeling?)

March 1845 *Blagdon*

As I am in bed you must not expect any beautiful writing. As I get better the Doctors treat me more and more like an invalid. "My cough is much diminished"—"Very good, you had better not go downstairs at all for fear of draughts. You must stay in bed till four p.m. and you are to have a liniment to cause an eruption on the top of the chest and thereby to take away every atom of irritation there

[1] Sydney Smith died in London on 22 February 1845.

may be inside." As soon as my cough is quite gone, I suppose I shall stay in bed *all* day. I think in the whole affair Mr. Dawson has rather taken the bull by the tail instead of the horns. I am *really* better, stronger and my cough *much* less. I now never cough from the time I go to bed till seven or eight in the morning. I have just eaten such a luncheon of partridge, your little puddings and calf's foot jelly without wine—do you approve? Also I now take isinglass in my tea, which they say is to make me strong. By the bye, I must tell you that Mrs. Bell means to go and see you, and I do not know whether I told you enough how very kind she was to me. You would have quite loved her if you had seen her taking care of me, and really I never saw anybody *except you* exert herself in the same way and seem so thoroughly interested.

The chicks are well except little Matt's leg which continues sore, but luckily he does not feel it. Mr. Dawson looks after it and says it is nothing. He said little Matt has become very disobedient since he has been so much upstairs. It cannot be my fancy, for even Wells and Heseltine remark it. It distresses me very much, for I cannot at present have them more with me—at least I think not, and yet I feel as if I was not doing my duty by them.

[The following letter, written about this time, is from Heseltine to Lady Parke:]

Thursday night at 8 o'clock   *Blagdon*

Madam, I am writing this beside Lady Ridley, during the time Sir Matthew has his dinner, and as I don't know whether Sir M. told your Ladyship that my beloved lady had a blister on yesterday and it rose beautifully and gave very little pain. Today it is stiff but no pain, which is a great blessing to me, and if I could speak to Lady R. just what I like I should not appear so stupid, but to feel restricted and afraid to say anything is very disagreeable, but it is as much as my place is worth to do so, therefore I must appear stupid to the end. Lady R. is certainly much better, but as to going out that will not be yet, for we have only had one day without an east wind, which will not do for a person that has been shut up so long, and today we have had sleet and rain and wind north east the whole day, but I shall set the village bells ringing the first day her Ladyship goes out, as I really think the air will assist to regain her strength. I sincerely hope it will not be long before we can try it. I am getting on well with the wrapper, considering I sit so little, and intend Lady Ridley to appear in it on Sunday next. I think it will look ladylike, and as it is Sir Matthew's choice it will be approved of. I write this in expectation of having such a character from Mr. Dawson tomorrow for being such a good nurse that I am afraid your Ladyship will say I am growing saucy, but knowing your hitherto kindness to me induces me to write just what I feel. Hoping your Ladyship will excuse the freedom, I beg to remain your Ladyship's ever dutiful and most obedient servant,

C. Heseltine.

I had sealed this in Lady R.'s dressing room and found the kind note from your Ladyship when I went into my room, and I hope your Ladyship will continue the notes, as her Ladyship looks forward to the post time with such pleasure and says to me after her dinner, which I am the only attendant at, "Now for the dessert," meaning your letter. Her Ladyship is weak in walking, her legs tremble from weakness, and does not gain any strength from the tonics. Your Ladyship may depend upon my increasing attention so long as I have strength, but I must say at present I am not so strong as I was. I sincerely wish you were here, but of course if Lady R. thought Sir Matthew would like it she would before now have asked it. He is extremely kind, not possible to be more so, but he has his peculiarities and will be obeyed. The children are quite well but wish we had a better tempered nurse, as there is no living with her on friendly terms.

March 1845   *Blagdon*

Dearest Mama, Heseltine told you of my bad day, when I went to bed and was so happy directly. I am strong today and comfortable, only very weak, which is such a bore. Yesterday I was virtuous enough to apply the liniment without being told. I expected great praise but was only told that I was quite right. It is oil of croton— the strongest essence of it that can be made. The doctors came yesterday in the afternoon to see how I looked when out of bed and dressed. They made me walk to *show off* and were much pleased with my performance. They are very attentive and seem quite interested in the case, but they do not expect me to be quite well and strong so long as this weather lasts. They are anxious I should not lose ground but do not expect much more strength.

[From now on all Lady Parke's letters to Cecilia have been preserved. She probably burnt earlier ones, but was at this stage too ill to do so.]

2 April 1845   *Ampthill*
My darling Cecilia, I should be quite happy at this dear Ampthill if I thought you were feeling more comfortable. I never felt comfortable until I sponged with salt and water and vinegar, but I daresay that would not be right for you now. Camphor julip used to quiet me and a little sal volatile in it. This lovely day ought to do good and I hope and trust and believe it will. We have been this morning to see the villagers and all are well excepting Gibbs and Forfeit, poor old women, I fear age is their chief ailment. Old Forfeit complained but cheered up and asked how you were. I said you had been ill but I hoped you would soon be better. She said "Hope's a good thing. Without hope hearts would break." We are to open our new school on the 24th and it will be a grand affair. We shall have many of the clergy and as many as choose to come to such a sight.

I have heard of two nurses and one of them has been four years with Mrs. Arthur Duncombe, who I suspect keeps her servants in good order. Mrs. Antrobus's nurse is also to be had, and when I receive their answers you shall have them and negotiate either by yourself or by Lady Ridley if you think it best and safest to do so. But as a good nurse slips through one's fingers I do not think I should lose a moment in making enquiries. I have told Lady Antrobus all about your quiet life, that she may judge how far it would suit Mrs. King.

10 April 1845   *Blagdon*
Dearest Papa, I must write you a small note to tell you that I have had a very comfortable good day and feel rather *up*. It is a curious

life that I lead—something like an enchanted Princess waiting to be delivered from her captivity by a valiant knight in the shape of a fine day. My captivity, however, is very pleasant and I have no bad fairies to tease me, unless I consider them as contained in the bottles of liniments with which I am so often tormented. I enjoy my books and the privilege of reading them so steadily, which is never the case when I am well. The chicks, too, are a great amusement to me, and would be more if it were not that they cause me to talk more than is right, so that I cannot have them with me as much as I should like. Little Matt can now tell me what he has been doing and sometimes speaks very distinctly. He is grown enormous and looks as well as possible and has many pictures of "Grandpapa" in his wig and gown. It is very nice to see them together—he is so gentle to "Masser Ecy" as he calls him, but still insists upon his rights, whilst Masser Ecy thinks nothing of giving his brother a good hit with his hand.

Mama really frightens me with her accounts of what she does—no peace or quiet for one minute. What a useful, active life she leads, and how different to mine now.

Goodbye, dearest Papa. Your very affectionate daughter,

C. Ridley.

[On 12 April, one week before she died, Cecilia wrote her last letter to her mother. For the first time her handwriting is rather shaky.]

Blagdon

Dearest Mama, I can really say that I am better now. My side is healed but still rather painful. The blister never was the slightest pain, but it chose to heal up entirely yesterday, and therefore I must have another, which is rather tiresome. For several days I have not been into my sitting room at all but remained in my dressing room and performed no toilet at all, which has agreed with me wonderfully. But today my wrapper is finished and I think I must dress a little and put it on. The worst of these blisters etc. is that I can wear no stays with them.

Now about nurses. I like the sound of the new one very much and shall be very anxious for you to see her. I am going to write to Lady

Ridley to tell her that I am going to part with Wells, and that if she hears of anyone likely to suit me I should be glad if she would let me know. I shall also ask her if she would object to my sending anyone to her in the meantime for her to see for me. She is so odd that she might be offended if it was done without notice. I think you had better not talk to her about it unless she begins. Do you know that I told 'Tine what was to happen? She expressed great joy and told me things that would have decided me long ago if I had known them. She says there is no doubt that temper is shown to the children and that she herself has seen her shake them violently. I think I shall write a description of the sort of nurse I like and send it to you to read to the nurse when you see her, or to any of them. Tell me if I am right in all this. Your very affectionate C. R.

I see I must put the affair in your hands. I should not like the nurse to slip away. Do you think it would be any good if you got her direction and I could write to her after your interview?

CHAPTER SEVENTEEN

Death

IT is not surprising in view of the tone of Cecilia's last letter that the Parkes were unaware how ill she really was. But their hopes must have been shattered by the following letter from Sir John Fife, the only one to survive, although it seems he had been in correspondence with the Baron all along.

17 April 1845   *Newcastle*
My dear Sir, Concluding that long before this you have received the letter I sent to you on the 12th to Ampthill, I have again delayed answering yours of the 14th and for the same reason as before.

Lady Ridley is if anything better than she was a few days ago, but there is no decisive change; anxious as I am to allay your apprehensions, I cannot hold out more sanguine hopes than before, yet so long as there is an expectation of pregnancy there is a probability of recovery.

Were the symptoms either greatly diminished or aggravated so as to change our present suspense into confident hope or absolute despair Lady Ridley would then probably see you and all her nearest and dearest friends: at present the least excitement raises her pulse from 86 to 120. There is one great consolation I can offer you—the tenderness and assiduity of Sir M. Ridley to his Lady is such that I never in the whole course of my experience saw equalled, and more than once after his manners in her presence have been cheerful and composed I have observed him break down and betray the keenest anguish on leaving her room: every little want seems anticipated and her wishes appear to direct and rule him. I remain, dear Sir James very truly yours, John Fife.

[Her condition deteriorated rapidly after this, and she must have developed an empyema or abscess on the pleural cavity. The Baron and Lady Parke were sent for, but did not arrive in time, receiving this letter from Sir Matthew after they had started:]

Sunday 20 April 1845   *Blagdon*
Dear Lady Parke,

All is alas over. I have thought it better thus to prepare you but briefly. My loved wife and your loved daughter has resigned her pure spirit at 8 min: past 10 this morning to that Almighty Power which gave it. I have thought it best to send this to meet you if I can at the railway station. Now I can write no more.

Affectionately yours, M. W. R.

In his journal he wrote that night:

It pleased God this day to take away from me my beloved wife, Cecilia Anne. She expired after an illness of about four months which she bore with exemplary patience at 8 minutes past 10 a.m. on Sunday morning. On Sat. 19th I was informed by her medical attendants Sir John Fife and Mr. W. Dawson that her eventual recovery was not to be expected. They did not however then expect so early a dissolution.

Her illness appeared to have proceeded from some long and very deeply seated disease of the lungs. Very occult and which gathered head with wonderful obstinacy in 4 months. The earlier stage of her attack was bronchitis—the immediate cause of her death effusion of mucus on the chest. "God's will be done" were her last words on earth.

To his own mother he wrote a much more detailed description:

I read to her and prayed with her at intervals. At one period she said "Pray for us." I did so in the natural expression of the emotion of our minds. I called her attention before midnight to what I told her I held her worse condition, that is that I thought her more ill, very ill. She said in reply "Is he (meaning Dawson) afraid for me?" I replied he thought her extremely ill and was so. I expressed strongly on her my own painful anticipations. I had told her in the afternoon of Saturday, previous to Mr. Dawson's second visit, that I had written to her mother and father saying she was considered worse, and that I thought she would like to see them, or rather her mother. She said "Very much." For the last few days she had not asked for the children, that is to see them. In the course of the night she seemed to dream occasionally, but the only words that I ever distinguished were these: "Among some of the villages." At or about midnight she seemed particularly ill. I enquired of Dawson whether I could with safety have the children brought down to her. He said he thought the excitement at that moment could not be hazarded. It was previous to her saying to me "Pray for us" that I for the first time seemed to have effectually impressed her situation on her. She asked once or twice for a psalm to be read. I read them to her. On asking what prayers I should read with her she said "The Lord's Prayer," and after one or two other prayers that she could not bear more. Then at six I asked her if I should read some of the Bible. She said "Yes." I asked her if she would like the chapter of Lazarus and of St. John. She said "Very much." I read about half of it with difficulty. Mr. Dawson was present. Hearing my voice falter much she said "You shall read no more, dear, go and get me that favourite bit of Gray: his *Ode on Vicissitude*." Immediately on my return Mr. Dawson left the room and I finished the chapter of Lazarus. When I finished she was dozing. Shortly after she said: "Now you shall tell me about the farm, I want to know all about it." I told her I had been there a few days ago but that on the previous day I had walked a little with the children, wishing to bring this matter round to arrest her attention. Shortly after this she became apparently worse, but not much so; about twenty minutes before her departure we had previously prayed together for all near and dear to us, and we expressed our submission to the Divine Will, she following me in my words apparently with the motion of her lips.

We took leave of each other as partners in joy and sorrow in this world, and with fervent prayer that we might meet hereafter in another. May God of His infinite mercy grant it be so. Previous to this I expressed a hope that it was possible her parents might arrive. She said she thought they could not, and that now, as she was, she did not think she would wish to live if she could. Mr. Dawson and I are not quite agreed as to what she said at this moment, he seeming to take it as though she could not wish to live for them to see her so ill, and I rather as though she would think her dissolution a release from this to a better world. "I trust," she said at one time, "that I am reconciled with my God." And at one moment, that she was now impatient, weary of lingering here below. I mentioned her children. She said she thought she had about time to see them. She embraced them at my earnest request, placed her hands upon each of their heads, blessed them. Wells brought the little girl, then the two boys. She pressed Wells's hand, the children were taken out. The light did not allow of their seeing sufficient to alarm, even the eldest. They little know what they have lost: in after life they must feel it. The eldest may retain a dream of having seen something good which he loved and that was good to him, and I pray he may, but by the Almighty's all wise dispensation he can have no more.

After the children were gone Cecilia said but little more. We again took leave of each other and she imperfectly but distinctly articulated "God's will be done." She took leave of Dawson, said "Thank you Mr. Dawson, thank you," very distinctly. In the course of the night she expressed a wish to be left entirely alone. Mr. Dawson then left the room and she begged me to sit in the corner, which I did for twenty minutes. I then resumed my place by her. At eight minutes past ten departed this life as pure and virtuous a being as ever existed. May that Almighty Power that took my blessed wife to Him this day so make me to bear this loss and affliction and so support and solace her parents and relations in the belief that through the mediation of our Blessed Saviour she may have been accepted by the God who created her.

Sir Matthew never married again. Indeed he never sufficiently recovered from Cecilia's death even to mention her name to the children until the end of his life. He lived on alone at Blagdon, becoming more and more absorbed in the farm, the estate and the breeding of prize cattle. But his life must have been lonely and friendless, and although he was a conscientious and affectionate father, it was many years before the children could be companions to him. In 1859, much to everyone's surprise, he decided to stand for Parliament, and was elected for the Northern Division of Northumberland, thus restoring the continuity of the Ridley representation in the House of Commons which he had severed at his father's death. He died on 25 September 1877, following a fall from the roof of a farm at the Morpeth Lunatic Asylum which he was inspecting.

In spite of Cecilia's fluctuating and at last decisive resolution to get rid of Wells, she stayed on with the children for another three years. I suppose that Sir Matthew was not worried by her day-to-day bad temper and moods and felt that he could confidently leave the health and well-being of the children in her harsh but competent hands. That Cecilia would have been unhappy at her staying on is quite clear, but what she would have minded far more was the fact that Sir Matthew fell out with Lord and Lady Parke and never spoke to them, nor were they allowed to see the children, until both the boys were about to leave Harrow. What the quarrel was about I have been unable to discover. All mention of it has evidently been destroyed. I thought it might have been because Sir Matthew and Sir John Fife prevented the Parkes from coming north to see Cecilia during her illness, but they came for the funeral and parted after that with kindness and affectionate notes on each side. Perhaps Lady Parke tried to interfere and dismiss Wells and take the children. Sir Matthew was always touchy and quick to take offence, and I suspect that his mother had something to do with it, and they may both have been jealous of Cecilia's devotion to her family. But whatever it was I doubt now if I shall ever find the cause. The fact remains that the children never saw their grandparents and were brought up in total ignorance of their existence until their last year at Harrow in 1860.

They had a very lonely and severe childhood. Wells was succeeded by a series of tutors for the boys, and governesses for Mary. She probably suffered the most from the effects of her mother's death. Her many governesses irritated her father to distraction, and she was, I fear, a very plain, dull girl with none of her mother's vitality and charm. She had, moreover, a glass eye, having been found, at the age of eight, to be blind in one eye. The discovery was made by Mr. Dawson, and one can almost hear him reassuring Sir Matthew that it was of no importance. The eye was removed by Dr. Bowman, a well-known eye surgeon in London, and Edward naïvely remarks in his memoirs that "in spite of this dreadful drawback Mary could always sketch with great effect and with the help of glasses could manage to put in distant effects." She married, in 1876, the Rev. Arthur Medd, Rector of Amble, and spent a life with him which ideally suited her deeply religious nature.

Both the boys had brilliant academic careers, and "little Matt" in particular distinguished himself at Harrow as the best classical scholar in the school. He was head of the school and when he won a Balliol scholarship and went up to Oxford he was succeeded in that capacity by Edward, a unique occurrence in the history of the school. The Annual Speech Day of 1860, when Matt won the school hexameter prize and also the school poem, was the occasion of a reconciliation with the Parkes, or rather with Lord and Lady Wensleydale, as they had then become. Lady Wensleydale described the event in a letter to Miss Fanny Barlow:

30 June 1860   *56 Park Street*

I am sure you will be interested in hearing about Harrow, where we went on Thursday to hear the speeches and dear Matt Ridley was the great interest of the day. He is a fine, manly looking fellow and his manner and style quite satisfactory, his speaking excellent and his abilities undoubted. He had six prizes, half of the whole, and he ended by speaking his own lines on Florence. It was very beautifully done and the applause was general. Lord Palmerston and all the people congratulated the Baron, and people said that the Baron's talents were coming out in him. The young ladies Villiers said how handsome he is and how beautiful his poem is. You will be surprised to hear that a kind of reconciliation took place between us and Sir Matthew, as far as shaking hands, and he said he would come to see me. There is little to be said or felt about him, but as a hope of seeing the children it is everything to us, for I never wished them to come here without the consent of their father. Edward is grown, but he looks less strong than Matt. Sir Matthew said he was as good as his brother and as clever. He seemed a nice boy. I tipped him and so did the Baron, and he looked quite surprised at my doing so. I don't quite see who Matt is like—I think between Mary and his mother. He has a good open forehead and a face you would like to look upon. He is sure to be a distinguished man. The Baron's happiness was intense. Mr. Holland told me he heard only good of him and that the boys praised him as much as the masters, which is remarkable. He is a good cricketer and he does not look worn by study. He had prizes for Latin, Greek, French and English.

[The two boys had equally distinguished careers at Oxford, where Edward took a Corpus Christi Scholarship the year after Matt went up. In 1868, when Sir Matthew retired, Matt was elected Member for North Northumberland without opposition. He had a far more distinguished political career than any of his forebears, being Home Secretary under Lord Salisbury in 1895. But in a reshuffle of the Government in 1900 he was asked to resign and created a Viscount, when he took as his second title that of his grandfather Lord Wensleydale, who had died in 1868. He married in 1873 Mary Georgiana Marjoribanks, a very charming and beautiful woman by whom he had two sons and three daughters.

Edward was called to the bar and eventually became a judge, though he never attained the eminence of Lord Wensleydale. He married Alice Bromley Davenport and had two sons.

Finally, it is nice to know what happened to Heseltine—"dear, devoted 'Tine." There is a letter from her preserved among the rest, written to Lady Parke in August 1845 from Stockport Court:]

Madam, As your Ladyship was so extremely kind in wishing to hear of my welfare I write to say I like Lady Georgina very much so far, and I think I can suit her Ladyship. . . . I hope that your Ladyship and Miss Parke have enjoyed your tour and that your Ladyship is restored to that tranquillity of mind which only the true Christian can feel, and that I am sure your Ladyship is in every sense of the word. But when I think of the past it seems like a dream until my duty reminds me I have work to perform for another which I was so proud to do for her who is now in the regions of bliss which can never be taken away from her.

Index

209